BONNIE*S
Household Budget Book

The Essential Workbook for Getting Control of Your Money

Newly Revised and Updated Edition

BONNIE RUNYAN McCULLOUGH

ST. MARTIN'S GRIFFIN ✴ NEW YORK

ALSO BY THE AUTHOR:

Totally Organized
Bonnie's Household Organizer
401 Ways to Get Your Kids to Work at Home
    (with Susan Monson)
76 Ways to Get Organized for Christmas
    (with Bev Cooper)

ACKNOWLEDGMENTS

Special thanks go to Barbara Anderson, my editor at St.
Martin's Press; to my special friend, Glenna Hansen Berg,
for being my sounding board, tutor and editor at home; to
my husband, Robert, my three daughters, Bobette, Laura,
and Becky, and my two sons, Wesley and Madison.

BONNIES HOUSEHOLD BUDGET BOOK, NEWLY REVISED
AND UPDATED EDITION. Copyright © 1981, 1983, 1987, 1992, 1995,
by Bonnie Runyan McCullough. All rights reserved. Printed in
the United States of America. No part of this book may
be used or reproduced in any manner whatsoever without
written permission except in the case of brief quotations
embodied in critical articles or reviews. For information,
address St. Martin's Press, 175 Fifth Avenue,
New York, N.Y. 10010.

Design by Mina Greenstein

Library of Congress Cataloging-in-Publication Data

McCullough, Bonnie Runyan.
    Bonnie's household budget book : the essential guide for getting
control of your money / by Bonnie Runyan McCullough.—4th rev. ed.
        p.   cm.
    ISBN 0-312-14098-3
    1. Home economics—Accounting.   I. Title.
TX326.M23   1996
640'.42—dc20
                                                                95-36219
                                                                CIP

Fourth Revised Edition

Contents

1996

JANUARY
```
S  M  T  W  T  F  S
      1  2  3  4  5  6
 7  8  9 10 11 12 13
14 15 16 17 18 19 20
21 22 23 24 25 26 27
28 29 30 31
```

FEBRUARY
```
S  M  T  W  T  F  S
            1  2  3
 4  5  6  7  8  9 10
11 12 13 14 15 16 17
18 19 20 21 22 23 24
25 26 27 28 29
```

MARCH
```
S  M  T  W  T  F  S
               1  2
 3  4  5  6  7  8  9
10 11 12 13 14 15 16
17 18 19 20 21 22 23
24 25 26 27 28 29 30
31
```

APRIL
```
S  M  T  W  T  F  S
    1  2  3  4  5  6
 7  8  9 10 11 12 13
14 15 16 17 18 19 20
21 22 23 24 25 26 27
28 29 30
```

MAY
```
S  M  T  W  T  F  S
          1  2  3  4
 5  6  7  8  9 10 11
12 13 14 15 16 17 18
19 20 21 22 23 24 25
26 27 28 29 30 31
```

JUNE
```
S  M  T  W  T  F  S
                  1
 2  3  4  5  6  7  8
 9 10 11 12 13 14 15
16 17 18 19 20 21 22
23 24 25 26 27 28 29
30
```

JULY
```
S  M  T  W  T  F  S
    1  2  3  4  5  6
 7  8  9 10 11 12 13
14 15 16 17 18 19 20
21 22 23 24 25 26 27
28 29 30 31
```

AUGUST
```
S  M  T  W  T  F  S
            1  2  3
 4  5  6  7  8  9 10
11 12 13 14 15 16 17
18 19 20 21 22 23 24
25 26 27 28 29 30 31
```

SEPTEMBER
```
S  M  T  W  T  F  S
 1  2  3  4  5  6  7
 8  9 10 11 12 13 14
15 16 17 18 19 20 21
22 23 24 25 26 27 28
29 30
```

OCTOBER
```
S  M  T  W  T  F  S
       1  2  3  4  5
 6  7  8  9 10 11 12
13 14 15 16 17 18 19
20 21 22 23 24 25 26
27 28 29 30 31
```

NOVEMBER
```
S  M  T  W  T  F  S
                1  2
 3  4  5  6  7  8  9
10 11 12 13 14 15 16
17 18 19 20 21 22 23
24 25 26 27 28 29 30
```

DECEMBER
```
S  M  T  W  T  F  S
 1  2  3  4  5  6  7
 8  9 10 11 12 13 14
15 16 17 18 19 20 21
22 23 24 25 26 27 28
29 30 31
```

1997

JANUARY
```
S  M  T  W  T  F  S
          1  2  3  4
 5  6  7  8  9 10 11
12 13 14 15 16 17 18
19 20 21 22 23 24 25
26 27 28 29 30 31
```

FEBRUARY
```
S  M  T  W  T  F  S
                  1
 2  3  4  5  6  7  8
 9 10 11 12 13 14 15
16 17 18 19 20 21 22
23 24 25 26 27 28
```

MARCH
```
S  M  T  W  T  F  S
                  1
 2  3  4  5  6  7  8
 9 10 11 12 13 14 15
16 17 18 19 20 21 22
23 24 25 26 27 28 29
30 31
```

APRIL
```
S  M  T  W  T  F  S
       1  2  3  4  5
 6  7  8  9 10 11 12
13 14 15 16 17 18 19
20 21 22 23 24 25 26
27 28 29 30
```

MAY
```
S  M  T  W  T  F  S
             1  2  3
 4  5  6  7  8  9 10
11 12 13 14 15 16 17
18 19 20 21 22 23 24
25 26 27 28 29 30 31
```

JUNE
```
S  M  T  W  T  F  S
 1  2  3  4  5  6  7
 8  9 10 11 12 13 14
15 16 17 18 19 20 21
22 23 24 25 26 27 28
29 30
```

JULY
```
S  M  T  W  T  F  S
       1  2  3  4  5
 6  7  8  9 10 11 12
13 14 15 16 17 18 19
20 21 22 23 24 25 26
27 28 29 30 31
```

AUGUST
```
S  M  T  W  T  F  S
                1  2
 3  4  5  6  7  8  9
10 11 12 13 14 15 16
17 18 19 20 21 22 23
24 25 26 27 28 29 30
31
```

SEPTEMBER
```
S  M  T  W  T  F  S
    1  2  3  4  5  6
 7  8  9 10 11 12 13
14 15 16 17 18 19 20
21 22 23 24 25 26 27
28 29 30
```

OCTOBER
```
S  M  T  W  T  F  S
          1  2  3  4
 5  6  7  8  9 10 11
12 13 14 15 16 17 18
19 20 21 22 23 24 25
26 27 28 29 30 31
```

NOVEMBER
```
S  M  T  W  T  F  S
                  1
 2  3  4  5  6  7  8
 9 10 11 12 13 14 15
16 17 18 19 20 21 22
23 24 25 26 27 28 29
30
```

DECEMBER
```
S  M  T  W  T  F  S
    1  2  3  4  5  6
 7  8  9 10 11 12 13
14 15 16 17 18 19 20
21 22 23 24 25 26 27
28 29 30 31
```

1998

JANUARY
```
S  M  T  W  T  F  S
             1  2  3
 4  5  6  7  8  9 10
11 12 13 14 15 16 17
18 19 20 21 22 23 24
25 26 27 28 29 30 31
```

FEBRUARY
```
S  M  T  W  T  F  S
 1  2  3  4  5  6  7
 8  9 10 11 12 13 14
15 16 17 18 19 20 21
22 23 24 25 26 27 28
```

MARCH
```
S  M  T  W  T  F  S
 1  2  3  4  5  6  7
 8  9 10 11 12 13 14
15 16 17 18 19 20 21
22 23 24 25 26 27 28
29 30 31
```

APRIL
```
S  M  T  W  T  F  S
          1  2  3  4
 5  6  7  8  9 10 11
12 13 14 15 16 17 18
19 20 21 22 23 24 25
26 27 28 29 30
```

MAY
```
S  M  T  W  T  F  S
                1  2
 3  4  5  6  7  8  9
10 11 12 13 14 15 16
17 18 19 20 21 22 23
24 25 26 27 28 29 30
31
```

JUNE
```
S  M  T  W  T  F  S
    1  2  3  4  5  6
 7  8  9 10 11 12 13
14 15 16 17 18 19 20
21 22 23 24 25 26 27
28 29 30
```

JULY
```
S  M  T  W  T  F  S
          1  2  3  4
 5  6  7  8  9 10 11
12 13 14 15 16 17 18
19 20 21 22 23 24 25
26 27 28 29 30 31
```

AUGUST
```
S  M  T  W  T  F  S
                  1
 2  3  4  5  6  7  8
 9 10 11 12 13 14 15
16 17 18 19 20 21 22
23 24 25 26 27 28 29
30 31
```

SEPTEMBER
```
S  M  T  W  T  F  S
       1  2  3  4  5
 6  7  8  9 10 11 12
13 14 15 16 17 18 19
20 21 22 23 24 25 26
27 28 29 30
```

OCTOBER
```
S  M  T  W  T  F  S
             1  2  3
 4  5  6  7  8  9 10
11 12 13 14 15 16 17
18 19 20 21 22 23 24
25 26 27 28 29 30 31
```

NOVEMBER
```
S  M  T  W  T  F  S
 1  2  3  4  5  6  7
 8  9 10 11 12 13 14
15 16 17 18 19 20 21
22 23 24 25 26 27 28
29 30
```

DECEMBER
```
S  M  T  W  T  F  S
       1  2  3  4  5
 6  7  8  9 10 11 12
13 14 15 16 17 18 19
20 21 22 23 24 25 26
27 28 29 30 31
```

Introduction

Why a household budget book? Well, if you're like most people I know, you devote a lot of time and energy to making money—money that nowadays seems to disappear as soon as it reaches your pocket.

Everywhere I turn, I hear people say, "I never seem to have enough money," or "My paycheck keeps shrinking while the price of everything else is skyrocketing." Everyone seems to be feeling the inflation squeeze these days. They're finding it harder to save money; they're cutting back on vacations, postponing major spending on cars and furniture, and finding it more difficult to pay for the necessities—like food and utilities—that they need every day.

A budget book can't tell you how to earn more money, or where to invest it, but it *can* help you manage your money so that you can obtain more of the things you *really* want. By using a budget book, you'll be able to answer that one question that pops up every month—"Where does the money go?" By keeping all the pieces of your financial puzzle in one place, a budget book helps you to see exactly where the money has gone. It also helps relieve the tax-time jitters because, with a budget book, you have all your expenditures recorded in one place.

Budgeting can aid you in many ways. My own experience has shown that a budget book can help you:

- enjoy the anticipation of choosing and buying
- appreciate what you get
- make successes and misjudgments highly visible
- replace impulse buying with logical, planned spending
- peek into the future to predict both expenses and spending sprees
- improve mutual understanding as you work together toward goals
- control your money rather than have it control you
- take advantage of *true* bargains
- buy carefully so you aren't sorry afterwards
- most of all—form realistic expectations, thus providing *hope*

Living with a budget doesn't necessarily mean you have to account for every dime or deny yourself every pleasure (if so, what is life for?), but household financial planning will help you get *more* or what you really want. If you don't plan, you are a slave to your every whim.

How do you use this book? First, find out where you are financially by using the 8-Step Spending Plan. This will show you how to estimate—and how to balance—your income and your expenses. It will also show you how to reduce your debts, how to set specific goals, and how to adjust your budget to fit changing needs.

The budget plan for our family of seven has been adjusted many times over the last sixteen years, but we've always found a budget to be useful—in fact essential—in obtaining the things we wanted. As young marrieds, having saved enough money for tuition and books, my husband and I lived on $40 a week—without welfare! From our first real paying job we saved twenty-five percent of our income toward a house. We were able to do this because we set our goals, planned carefully, and kept our life simple. Another young married couple, during those same years, showed off their new freezer full of juices, TV-dinners, vegetables, and meat. "We only paid $1,000 for all of this" (plus interest charges for two years of installment payments). For that same $1,000, my husband and I bought not only a new freezer (same size as theirs but without food, for $300) but also a car (four years old), a dishwasher, and a washing machine. These kinds of decisions make a lot of difference in how quickly you can reach the standard of living you want and how much money you have left for the other pleasures of life. Setting up a plan and keeping a budget can be rewarding, not only financially but also mentally, if you use it as a guide, not as a beating stick.

In this book you'll also find monthly forms for keeping track of expenditures. You'll find places to keep tax records, information on how to use credit, and dozens of hints on saving money in specific areas such as food, transportation, entertainment, and home energy. For extra help, I have included ideas for involving the whole family in your spending plan, and a pep talk for cutting impulsive spending. As an added tool for your research, I have included a list of government bulletins. If all these fail to give you enough help solving your financial problems, seek professional help.

Many people think MORE money will solve their problems. I can't give you more money, but I can help you make the most of what you *do* have. Take time to plan your spending and the rewards will be more lasting. Remember:

Most unhappiness is caused by giving up what you want most for what you want at the moment.

Bonnie McCullough
Lakewood, Colorado

1
Estimate Yearly Income

Before you can decide where you would like to go, you have to decide where you are, and you start this by estimating your total income for the year. Include bonuses, commissions, interest, etc., if you get them. Windfall money such as gifts or income tax refunds can, if you desire, be put straight into savings or spent for a special purchase without being calculated into the monthly expense budget. If you anticipate getting a raise during the course of the year, your should base your calculations on your *present* salary, and then make adjustments after you get the raise.

People with irregular income should estimate the largest and smallest amounts likely to be available and use the smaller figure for the spending plan. They then should look at reserve funds they could draw on and expenditures that could be omitted if necessary.

*On the first line, enter the amount of income you receive *after* federal, state, and FICA taxes are withheld (net income). If your employer does not take out these withholdings, or if you have a lot of income other than regular wages, fill in your total income *before* taxes (gross income) and then be sure to do Step 2 or you could end up owing a large tax bill you had not planned for.

INCOME	AMOUNT
Salaries and Wages* (Net or Gross)	
Bonuses	
Commissions	
Interest	
Dividends	
Real Estate	
Money Gifts	
Tips	
Allowances	
Income Tax Refunds	
Benefit Payments	
Pensions	
Annuities	

Estimate
Withholdings

TAXES AND RETIREMENT	
Federal Taxes	
State Taxes	
Local Taxes	
FICA or Pension Plan	
Estimated Withholdings Yearly Total	

Total Estimated Gross Income		
Subtract Estimated Yearly Withholdings	−	
Estimate of Total Yearly Spendable Income		

If your employer does not withhold federal, state, local, and FICA taxes, use Step 2 to estimate how much money you should set aside for tax and retirement funds. To estimate your federal withholding tax, figure your gross yearly income (Step 1), then refer to last year's tax forms or the tax tables in last year's federal tax instruction booklet. Record the estimated tax in the box opposite. To figure state and local taxes, use your gross yearly income and the tax tables from last year's state tax instruction booklet. Record these two figures.

FICA is now made up of two separate taxes. For 1995, the Social Security (OASDI) tax rate is 6.2% of income up to $61,200. The Medicare tax rate is 1.45% of income, with no ceiling. If you are self-employed, a 15.3% tax is computed as follows: a 12.4% Social Security tax of income up to $61,200, and a 2.9% Medicare tax with no ceiling.

To figure your total spendable income, take the sum of all estimated taxes and subtract that amount from your gross income.

3

Estimate Fixed Expenses

Estimate your fixed expenses—those that do not vary much during the year. Plan how you will set aside money for once-a-year payments including house and car insurance, licenses, and taxes so that when these fixed expenses come due, you can pay them comfortably.

The emergency savings (rainy-day) fund is for items you must buy, but have not planned for because it is impossible to predict all future expenses. It is desirable to add a definite amount to this fund each pay period (some suggest 5%). A separate permanent savings fund is suggested (7–10% of total income) for sound money management.

This chart will give you a picture of how much of your income you have already committed. To figure how much money you will have left over for flexible living expenses, total the fixed expenses and subtract that number from your total yearly spendable income (Steps 1 & 2). Divide by twelve to see how much money you will have each month for flexible living espenses (see chart below). Perhaps, in the future, if this amount does not allow enough for comfortable daily living, you can review and change some of your commitments and avoid taking on so many installment payments and loans.

	Amount for year	Amount per month (divide yearly amt. by 12)
HOUSING		
Rent or Mortgage (PITI—Principal, Interest, Taxes, Insurance)		
Parking Garage or Space Rentals		
Condominium Association Membership		
PROTECTION		
Life Insurance		
Health Insurance		
Dental Insurance		
Car Insurance		
SAVINGS		
Investments		
Emergency Fund		
Permanent Fund		
Travel Fund		
DEBTS AND OBLIGATIONS		
Auto loan		
Installments		
PERSONAL IMPROVEMENT AND COMMUNITY (may be fixed)		
Church		
Union or Professional Dues		
Health Club Dues		
Tuitions		
Service Clubs		
OTHER MAJOR ITEMS		
Child support		
Alimony		

Total Yearly Spendable Income (Steps 1 + 2)	
Total Fixed Yearly Expenses −	
Yearly Spendable Income for Flexible Expenses	
Monthly Spendable Income for Flexible Expenses = (%12) =	

4

Estimate Flexible Living Expenses

HOUSING (other than fixed rent or mortgage)	Amount for year	Amount per month
Heat, Gas, Electricity, Water		
Telephone		
Trash removal		
Equipment		
Repairs		
TRANSPORTATION AND UPKEEP		
Gas		
Upkeep		
Public transportation		
FOOD AND SUNDRIES		
Groceries		
Quantity foods		
Meals away from home		
Paper and laundry products		
Toiletries		
CLOTHING AND SHOES (including care and repair)		
EDUCATION, LESSONS, BOOKS, MAGAZINES, PAPER, POSTAGE		
ENTERTAINMENT, RECREATION, GIFTS		
PAID SERVICES		
MEDICAL		
Dentist		
Doctor		
Medicines		
OTHER		
Contributions, if not fixed		

Estimate your average flexible living expenses by reviewing past bills and looking at records, receipts, and cancelled checks from last year. These areas of flexible expense will give you clues as to where money can be saved. After you have estimated the monthly budget, you will not know for sure if it is workable until you have kept careful records for several months.

If you are just starting out on your own, or entering marriage, or buying a new home and have no idea how to estimate these expenses, fill them in as best you can and then ask an experienced friend who lives in your neighborhood if your figures are realistic.

There are many tradeoffs in the area of flexible expenses. Refer to the tips beginning on page 51 for ways to cut down on expenses in specific categories. Keeping track of your spending for several months will help you understand whether you are spending by planning or by impulse. It isn't necessary to account for every single dime; but then those little expenses can add up—buying a can of soda from a dispenser every day at work can add up to nearly $250 in a year!

5
Balance Income and Outgo

☐ Very little left? Don't be discouraged! After a time, the experience you gain from using *Bonnie's Household Budget Book* should improve this situation. Don't forget, though, that people always want more than they have, thus the need for planning, management, and self-discipline. For more spendable cash, try Steps 6a and 6b.

☐ Expenses more than income? Don't quit. Sharpen your pencil and start now to MANAGE. You need Steps 6a and 6b.

☐ Is your income *more* than your expenses? Congratulations! (Now wait a minute, have you been realistic with your estimates or are you trying to pinch the dollars too tightly?) If you have more than you spend, you are doing great—just use this book to plan your goals and as an aid at income tax time.

Any surplus not accounted for may be used in any way you choose. Hopefully you will begin an investment and savings plan to prepare for retirement. You may move on to Step 7.

Estimated Total Yearly Spendable Income _____

Estimated Yearly Fixed Expenses _____

Estimated Yearly Flexible Living Expenses + _____

Total Expenses − _____

Plus or Minus

6a
Cutting Back

Look at all the ways to cut down on little things. Nowadays, a penny saved is worth two pennies earned because you lose so much of the earned penny to taxes and expenses. Go back over each of the flexible expense categories and cut back where possible, but be sure to leave at least a little something in each category (we need a few niceties today while we work toward tomorrow!) Cutting back too severely—especially on food and fun—builds discontentment with the whole budget idea and can cause you to break your budget and react by spending more than ever. If your budget is out of balance, don't take on any more fixed expenses at the present time. Instead, you should concentrate on cutting back flexible expenses first: food, clothing, entertainment, magazines, travel, gifts, etc.

If you live with others, discuss these sacrifices with them and ask where they are willing to cut back to spend less. Try some of the money-saving tips in the back of this book.

Name of Company	Approximate monthly payment	Yearly Service Charge	Amount Owed Creditor	How many months to eliminate this debt?
TOTALS				

6b
Cutting Back Consumer Debts

Take a good look at how much money you owe. Most people have never seen it listed and totaled in one place.

Cut down present debt. Your total debt can be reduced simply by continuing to pay monthly payments and by not charging anything more. This will be a real sacrifice—it means doing without and waiting for what you want. Take a look at your credit buying. (Do not include home mortgage.) List your personal credit obligations. Notice how much you are paying for service charges. This money could be yours.* And since the government no longer allows tax deductions for interest paid on consumer debt, you no longer have a tax benefit.

Set a date by which you will have paid those debts and will be free of their monthly payments. As each account is paid off, the money that was going for payment and interest charges is now yours—to save toward other goals or to accelerate payment of other debts.

By cutting back on flexible spending and concentrating on elimination of installment debt, more spendable income will become available for you. This exercise may be a little hard, but it is much easier to weigh the facts here and make your plans (that's why it is called *managing*) than to fret and get depressed after you have overspent. You can begin to exercise self-discipline and not "blow" money on unintended overspending. If, after you have tried this plan for a while, you still are juggling debts and spending more than you earn, perhaps it is time to seek professional financial counseling (see pages 45–46 for suggestions).

For some, there is a possibility of increasing income by moonlighting or sending the children or spouse to work. But remember, every job carries certain hidden costs—costs for taxes, transportation, clothing, food, daycare, and special help (to do the things you won't have time to do if you work). If you or someone in your family takes an extra job, calculate only the *spendable income* (not the *total salary*) from that job.

7

Set Goals

Now that you know where you are and how much money you actually have to spend, you can plan how best to save or spend it. This is an important step that all self-disciplined people use, and the one step that most people are inclined to skip. As you set up a budget and get everything together, you will probably think of things you would like to do with your money. Jot down these ideas. There will be short-term wants like a trip to Vegas or new wallpaper for the kitchen, and long-term wants like a new car, down payment on a house, or retirement. Reducing your debt to free up more money for daily spending may be your goal. For others, it may be just the opposite—cutting down on the leaks in daily spending in order to afford a large purchase.

If you have a family, call everyone together to discuss their wants and needs and to set goals. List everyone's ideas at this stage. Many goals take more than money; they take time and effort. Consider these preparations with your family, too.

Look over your list of goals and set your priorities. What do you want most? Which items can wait until next month or next year? If you don't have cash, you will want to set up a savings plan to meet your goals. You will need to consider UFO's (UnForeseen Obligations) for such things as house or car repairs and medical emergencies, and allow funds for desirable things like furniture, equipment, a new car, educational opportunities, vacations, holiday giving, major clothing purchases, or investments. Set aside a little money each month in your operational savings fund toward these goals. You may use one account for all three types of savings: 1) emergency fund, 2) operational fund for goals, and 3) permanent savings for long-range goals. Or you may have three separate savings accounts—almost like dividing cash into different envelopes.

Your goals will change. Write them down at least once a year—maybe in January or at tax time. Taking time to set goals will help keep your number one priorities in view; you won't be as likely to lose sight of them because of impulsive "see and buy" purchases.

GOALS Future Wants and Needs	Indicate When			Total Amount Needed	How will this goal be achieved? Save? Borrow? At what rate?
	This Year	Future (Number Years)	At retire-ment		

NET WORTH

ASSETS		LIABILITIES	
CASH		**Current Bills**	
Savings account			
Checking account			
Credit union			
Securities			
U.S. Bonds			
Other Bonds		**Bank Loans and Charge Accounts**	
Stocks (current market value)		Car	
CD's		Recreational vehicle	
Notes and Loans receivable		Credit cards	
		Charge accounts	
Real Estate—Market value			
		Real Estate Loans	
		House	
		Investment property	
Insurance Cash Value			
Other Property		**Other**	
Automobile (market value)		Taxes	
Jewelry; collections such as stamps and coins			
Furniture			
Equipment			
Tools			
Total Assets		**Total Liabilities**	
		TOTAL ASSETS	
		TOTAL LIABILITIES	
		NET WORTH	

8

Evaluate

After your plan is complete, you need to put it into action. On the monthly expense charts that follow, keep a record of what you are spending to see if you are spending as planned. Fill in the amounts spent in each of the categories. Take an hour at the end of the month to calculate totals and then add them to the summary charts starting on page 24. If you don't take time to evaluate, filling in charts is just busywork.

Planned spending can be a rewarding experience because it produces wiser spending habits and captures more of the loose change for better living. Reevaluate your spending plan often. Ask yourself:

- Did I stay within limits?
- Am I making progress toward my goals?
- Am I buying items I planned for?
- Are there still adjustments to be made?
- Do I feel successful?

At least once a year, figure your net worth by totaling assets and subtracting liabilities (debts and bills) as part of your evaluation. Also, plan a review of your financial goals and priorities at least once a year.

Explanation of Monthly Expense Sheet

(SEE CORRESPONDING NUMBERS ON OPPOSITE SAMPLE PAGE.)

1 Record the amount left in your checking account or cash on hand to calculate spendable income for this month. If the leftover amount is to be set aside for a future expense like car insurance, perhaps you will want to transfer it to your emergency savings account so it will not get spent for something else.

2 Estimate the amount budgeted for each category, filling in the box for each one. Refer to your original yearly estimate for comparison.

3 Record income as it is received, including money taken from savings for purchases or payments. Monies withheld from your paycheck for things like insurance, savings, or loan payments should be recorded in the appropriate column on the Monthly Expense Chart to have a true total of how much money is being spent in those categories.

For your financial safety, also record income totals and withholding figures on the Income Summary forms. This will help you double check employer's bookkeeping and provide accurate amounts at tax time.

4 Record the amounts spent in the appropriate columns during the month. A few people will need to do this every day, but for most, once a week is enough. If need be, write a one-word description above the amount. If you do not make daily entries in the Budget Book, keep receipts and make notes on a card in your wallet until you have time to write them in the Budget Book. When you pay for an item by check, note what it was for in the checkbook ledger. Cash withdrawals are especially hard to keep track of; record the purpose on the withdrawal receipt.

5 At the end of the month, total each column. Add these totals for the grand total of the month's expenses. Transfer the column totals to the yearly summary on page 27. When adding each month's expenses, take a minute to enter any tax deductible items in the appropriate deduction summaries (pages 28–30). It is much easier to do a few each month than to try and remember them all at tax time. Remember to keep the receipts from these items and have a specific place to keep them as suggested in the section on filing financial papers (page 42). To get a true picture of how much gas and electricity you use, fill in the utilities usage chart on page 34.

6 Subtract your total expenses from this month's cash to know what balance you have left. Evaluate the results and make any necessary adjustments.

MONTHLY EXPENSE CHART MONTH January YEAR _____

TAX CONSIDERATIONS (Keep Receipts)

Box 2 | **Box 3**

Column headers:
- Operational savings, emergency savings, permanent savings — **Save**
- Life insurance — **Life**
- Rent or mortgage — **House**
- Home upkeep, furnishings — **Upkeep**
- Gas, lights, water, phone, trash, sewer — **Util.**
- Transportation, auto upkeep, insurance — **Auto**
- Food, sundries, paper and laundry products — **Food**
- Clothing, shoes (care and repair) — **Cloth.**
- Allowances, grooming, personal expenses — **Pers.**
- Education, lessons, books, magazines, papers — **Ed.**
- Entertainment, recreation, gifts — **Fun**
- Services — **Serv.**
- Other — **Other**
- Contributions — **Give**
- Medicines, prescription drugs — **Drugs**
- Dentist, doctor, medical, health insurance — **Doc.**
- Interest, taxes, child care, losses, professional and business expenses — **Other**

AVAILABLE CASH* (income, savings withdrawals, dividends and interest, bonuses, and loan proceeds) — **Source / Amount**

Row	Save	Life	House	Upkeep	Util.	Auto	Food	Cloth.	Pers.	Ed.	Fun	Serv.	Other	Give	Drugs	Doc.	Other	Source	Amount
Amount Budgeted	300	35.28	810	60	130	612	660	100	200	40	100	85	60	40	60	330		Borgas Co.	1,801
1		35.28			101.10	19.80												Savings-Fed.	350
2		Western			19.20				2.25					40.00		55.72		SMP, Inc.	430
3			19.95		3.60		198.00						6.00			Dental		DMA, Inc.	407
4																6.19 Ins.		C+F, Inc.	456
5	155.00								40.00										
6	Credit							65.00			12.00	15.00					17.01		
7	Union		174.00			12.00		L. Shoes				baby					Visa Interest		
8			1st Nat				18.00					sitter							
9																			
10										17.00						226.85			
11	90.00									News						Kaiser			
12	Vacation		636.00		14.40		19.00	40.00					7.00			Ins.			
13	Fund		Cap.				42.10	blk shirt								7.63			
14			Fund																
15					71.10														
16					Ins.						7.00								
17							210.00												
18	55.00																		
19	Christmas							16.00	40.00										
20	Fund			12.16				Kathy											
21					33.60											10.80			
22												31.20							
23					7.50							spray				18.00			
24									3.00			trees				Dr. Berg			
25							7.00		3.00										
26					15.00			Socks			22.00		29.50						
27							162.00												
28																			
29					420.00				27.00										
30					loan				hair										
31																			
TOTALS	300	35.28	810	32.11	123.90	593.40	630	107	155.25	17	41	46.20	42.50	40	24.62	300.57	17.01		

Total cash this month **3,444**

Boxes 1, 4, 5, 6 (marked on form)

MONTHLY SUMMARY

Last month's cash brought forward	39.28
This month's cash +	3,444.00
Total	3,483.28
Subtract total expenses this month −	3,315.84
BALANCE FORWARD	**167.44**

* Record income tax and retirement withholdings on income summary page 24.
Other payroll withholdings should be recorded in the appropriate columns on this monthly expense form.

MONTHLY EXPENSE CHART

MONTH _____ YEAR _____

	Operational savings, emergency savings, permanent savings	Life insurance	Rent or mortgage	Home upkeep, furnishings	Gas, lights, water, phone, trash, sewer	Transportation, auto upkeep, insurance	Food, sundries, paper and laundry products	Clothing, shoes (care and repair)	Allowances, grooming, personal expenses	Education, lessons, books, magazines, papers	Entertainment, recreation, gifts	Services	Other	TAX CONSIDERATIONS (Keep Receipts)				AVAILABLE CASH* (income, savings withdrawals, dividends and interest, bonuses, and loan proceeds)	
														Contributions	Medicines, prescription drugs	Dentist, doctor, medical, health insurance	Interest, taxes, child care, losses, professional and business expenses		
	Save	Life	House	Upkeep	Util.	Auto	Food	Cloth.	Pers.	Ed.	Fun	Serv.	Other	Give	Drugs	Doc.	Other	Source	Amount
Amount Budgeted																			
1																			
2																			
3																			
4																			
5																			
6																			
7																			
8																			
9																			
10																			
11																			
12																			
13																			
14																			
15																			
16																			
17																			Total cash this month
18																			
19																			
20																			
21																			
22																			MONTHLY SUMMARY
23																			Last month's cash brought forward _____
24																			
25																			This month's cash + _____
26																			
27																			Total _____
28																			Subtract total expenses this month − _____
29																			
30																			
31																			
TOTALS																			BALANCE FORWARD

12

Enter totals on summary page 27

* Record income tax and retirement withholdings on income summary page 24.
Other payroll withholdings should be recorded in the appropriate columns on this monthly expense form.

MONTHLY EXPENSE CHART

MONTH _____ YEAR _____

	Operational savings, emergency savings, permanent savings	Life insurance	Rent or mortgage	Home upkeep, furnishings	Gas, lights, water, phone, trash, sewer	Transportation, auto upkeep, insurance	Food, sundries, paper and laundry products	Clothing, shoes (care and repair)	Allowances, grooming, personal expenses	Education, lessons, books, magazines, papers	Entertainment, recreation, gifts	Services	Other	TAX CONSIDERATIONS (Keep Receipts)				AVAILABLE CASH* (income, savings withdrawals, dividends and interest, bonuses, and loan proceeds)	
														Contributions	Medicines, prescription drugs	Dentist, doctor, medical, health insurance	Interest, taxes, child care, losses, professional and business expenses		
	Save	Life	House	Upkeep	Util.	Auto	Food	Cloth.	Pers.	Ed.	Fun	Serv.	Other	Give	Drugs	Doc.	Other	Source	Amount
Amount Budgeted																			
1																			
2																			
3																			
4																			
5																			
6																			
7																			
8																			
9																			
10																			
11																			
12																			
13																			
14																			
15																			
16																			
17																			
18																			
19																			
20																			
21																			
22																			
23																			
24																			
25																			
26																			
27																			
28																			
29																			
30																			
31																			
TOTALS																			

Total cash this month

MONTHLY SUMMARY

Last month's cash brought forward _____

This month's cash + _____

Total _____

Subtract total expenses this month − _____

BALANCE FORWARD

Enter totals on summary page 27

* Record income tax and retirement withholdings on income summary page 24.
Other payroll withholdings should be recorded in the appropriate columns on this monthly expense form.

13

MONTHLY EXPENSE CHART   MONTH _____ YEAR _____

	Operational savings, emergency savings, permanent savings	Life insurance	Rent or mortgage	Home upkeep, furnishings	Gas, lights, water, phone, trash, sewer	Transportation, auto upkeep, insurance	Food, sundries, paper and laundry products	Clothing, shoes (care and repair)	Allowances, grooming, personal expenses	Education, lessons, books, magazines, papers	Entertainment, recreation, gifts	Services	Other	TAX CONSIDERATIONS (Keep Receipts)				AVAILABLE CASH* (income, savings withdrawals, dividends and interest, bonuses, and loan proceeds)	
														Contributions	Medicines, prescription drugs	Dentist, doctor, medical, health insurance	Interest, taxes, child care, losses, professional and business expenses		
	Save	Life	House	Upkeep	Util.	Auto	Food	Cloth.	Pers.	Ed.	Fun	Serv.	Other	Give	Drugs	Doc.	Other	Source	Amount
Amount Budgeted																			
1																			
2																			
3																			
4																			
5																			
6																			
7																			
8																			
9																			
10																			
11																			
12																			
13																			
14																			
15																			
16																			
17																			
18																			
19																			
20																			
21																			
22																			
23																			
24																			
25																			
26																			
27																			
28																			
29																			
30																			
31																			
TOTALS																			

Total cash this month

MONTHLY SUMMARY

Last month's cash brought forward _____

This month's cash + _____

Total _____

Subtract total expenses this month − _____

BALANCE FORWARD

Enter totals on summary page 27

* Record income tax and retirement withholdings on income summary page 24.
Other payroll withholdings should be recorded in the appropriate columns on this monthly expense form.

MONTHLY EXPENSE CHART   MONTH _____   YEAR _____

	Operational savings, emergency savings, permanent savings	Life insurance	Rent or mortgage	Home upkeep, furnishings	Gas, lights, water, phone, trash, sewer	Transportation, auto upkeep, insurance	Food, sundries, paper and laundry products	Clothing, shoes (care and repair)	Allowances, grooming, personal expenses	Education, lessons, books, magazines, papers	Entertainment, recreation, gifts	Services	Other	TAX CONSIDERATIONS (Keep Receipts)				AVAILABLE CASH* (income, savings withdrawals, dividends and interest, bonuses, and loan proceeds)	
														Contributions	Medicines, prescription drugs	Dentist, doctor, medical, health insurance	Interest, taxes, child care, losses, professional and business expenses		
	Save	Life	House	Upkeep	Util.	Auto	Food	Cloth.	Pers.	Ed.	Fun	Serv.	Other	Give	Drugs	Doc.	Other	Source	Amount
Amount Budgeted																			
1																			
2																			
3																			
4																			
5																			
6																			
7																			
8																			
9																			
10																			
11																			
12																			
13																			
14																			
15																			
16																			
17																			
18																			
19																			
20																			
21																			
22																			
23																			
24																			
25																			
26																			
27																			
28																			
29																			
30																			
31																			
TOTALS																			

Total cash this month ☐

MONTHLY SUMMARY

Last month's cash brought forward _____

This month's cash   + _____

Total _____

Subtract total expenses this month   − _____

BALANCE FORWARD

Enter totals on summary page 27

* Record income tax and retirement withholdings on income summary page 24.
Other payroll withholdings should be recorded in the appropriate columns on this monthly expense form.

15

MONTHLY EXPENSE CHART   MONTH _____ YEAR _____

	Operational savings, emergency savings, permanent savings	Life insurance	Rent or mortgage	Home upkeep, furnishings	Gas, lights, water, phone, trash, sewer	Transportation, auto upkeep, insurance	Food, sundries, paper and laundry products	Clothing, shoes (care and repair)	Allowances, grooming, personal expenses	Education, lessons, books, magazines, papers	Entertainment, recreation, gifts	Services	Other	TAX CONSIDERATIONS (Keep Receipts)				AVAILABLE CASH* (income, savings withdrawals, dividends and interest, bonuses, and loan proceeds)	
														Contributions	Medicines, prescription drugs	Dentist, doctor, medical, health insurance	Interest, taxes, child care, losses, professional and business expenses		
	Save	Life	House	Upkeep	Util.	Auto	Food	Cloth.	Pers.	Ed.	Fun	Serv.	Other	Give	Drugs	Doc.	Other	Source	Amount
Amount Budgeted																			
1																			
2																			
3																			
4																			
5																			
6																			
7																			
8																			
9																			
10																			
11																			
12																			
13																			
14																			
15																			
16																			
17																			Total cash this month
18																			
19																			
20																			
21																			
22																			MONTHLY SUMMARY
23																			Last month's cash brought forward
24																			
25																			This month's cash +
26																			
27																			Total
28																			Subtract total expenses this month −
29																			
30																			
31																			
TOTALS																			BALANCE FORWARD

Enter totals on summary page 27

* Record income tax and retirement withholdings on income summary page 24.
Other payroll withholdings should be recorded in the appropriate columns on this monthly expense form.

MONTHLY EXPENSE CHART

MONTH _____ YEAR _____

	Operational savings, emergency savings, permanent savings	Life insurance	Rent or mortgage	Home upkeep, furnishings	Gas, lights, water, phone, trash, sewer	Transportation, auto upkeep, insurance	Food, sundries, paper and laundry products	Clothing, shoes (care and repair)	Allowances, grooming, personal expenses	Education, lessons, books, magazines, papers	Entertainment, recreation, gifts	Services	Other	TAX CONSIDERATIONS (Keep Receipts)				AVAILABLE CASH* (income, savings withdrawals, dividends and interest, bonuses, and loan proceeds)	
														Contributions	Medicines, prescription drugs	Dentist, doctor, medical, health insurance	Interest, taxes, child care, losses, professional and business expenses		
	Save	Life	House	Upkeep	Util.	Auto	Food	Cloth.	Pers.	Ed.	Fun	Serv.	Other	Give	Drugs	Doc.	Other	Source	Amount
Amount Budgeted																			
1																			
2																			
3																			
4																			
5																			
6																			
7																			
8																			
9																			
10																			
11																			
12																			
13																			
14																			
15																			
16																			
17																			
18																			
19																			
20																			
21																			
22																			
23																			
24																			
25																			
26																			
27																			
28																			
29																			
30																			
31																			
TOTALS																			

Total cash this month [ ]

MONTHLY SUMMARY

Last month's cash brought forward _____

This month's cash + _____

Total _____

Subtract total expenses this month − _____

BALANCE FORWARD

Enter totals on summary page 27

* Record income tax and retirement withholdings on income summary page 24.
Other payroll withholdings should be recorded in the appropriate columns on this monthly expense form

MONTHLY EXPENSE CHART

MONTH _____ YEAR _____

	Operational savings, emergency savings, permanent savings	Life insurance	Rent or mortgage	Home upkeep, furnishings	Gas, lights, water, phone, trash, sewer	Transportation, auto upkeep, insurance	Food, sundries, paper and laundry products	Clothing, shoes (care and repair)	Allowances, grooming, personal expenses	Education, lessons, books, magazines, papers	Entertainment, recreation, gifts	Services	Other	TAX CONSIDERATIONS (Keep Receipts)				AVAILABLE CASH* (income, savings withdrawals, dividends and interest, bonuses, and loan proceeds)	
														Contributions	Medicines, prescription drugs	Dentist, doctor, medical, health insurance	Interest, taxes, child care, losses, professional and business expenses		
	Save	Life	House	Upkeep	Util.	Auto	Food	Cloth.	Pers.	Ed.	Fun	Serv.	Other	Give	Drugs	Doc.	Other	Source	Amount
Amount Budgeted																			
1																			
2																			
3																			
4																			
5																			
6																			
7																			
8																			
9																			
10																			
11																			
12																			
13																			
14																			
15																			
16																			
17																			Total cash this month
18																			
19																			
20																			
21																			
22																			MONTHLY SUMMARY
23																			Last month's cash brought forward _____
24																			
25																			This month's cash + _____
26																			
27																			Total _____
28																			Subtract total expenses this month − _____
29																			
30																			
31																			
TOTALS																			BALANCE FORWARD

Enter totals on summary page 27

* Record income tax and retirement withholdings on income summary page 24.
Other payroll withholdings should be recorded in the appropriate columns on this monthly expense form.

MONTHLY EXPENSE CHART   MONTH _____   YEAR _____

	Operational savings, emergency savings, permanent savings	Life insurance	Rent or mortgage	Home upkeep, furnishings	Gas, lights, water, phone, trash, sewer	Transportation, auto upkeep, insurance	Food, sundries, paper and laundry products	Clothing, shoes (care and repair)	Allowances, grooming, personal expenses	Education, lessons, books, magazines, papers	Entertainment, recreation, gifts	Services	Other	TAX CONSIDERATIONS (Keep Receipts)				AVAILABLE CASH* (income, savings withdrawals, dividends and interest, bonuses, and loan proceeds)	
														Contributions	Medicines, prescription drugs	Dentist, doctor, medical, health insurance	Interest, taxes, child care, losses, professional and business expenses		
	Save	Life	House	Upkeep	Util.	Auto	Food	Cloth.	Pers.	Ed.	Fun	Serv.	Other	Give	Drugs	Doc.	Other	Source	Amount
Amount Budgeted																			
1																			
2																			
3																			
4																			
5																			
6																			
7																			
8																			
9																			
10																			
11																			
12																			
13																			
14																			
15																			
16																			
17																			
18																			
19																			
20																			
21																			
22																			
23																			
24																			
25																			
26																			
27																			
28																			
29																			
30																			
31																			
TOTALS																			

Total cash this month [ ]

MONTHLY SUMMARY

Last month's cash brought forward _____

This month's cash + _____

Total _____

Subtract total expenses this month − _____

BALANCE FORWARD

Enter totals on summary page 27

* Record income tax and retirement withholdings on income summary page 24.
Other payroll withholdings should be recorded in the appropriate columns on this monthly expense form.

19

MONTHLY EXPENSE CHART   MONTH _____ YEAR _____

	Operational savings, emergency savings, permanent savings	Life insurance	Rent or mortgage	Home upkeep, furnishings	Gas, lights, water, phone, trash, sewer	Transportation, auto upkeep, insurance	Food, sundries, paper and laundry products	Clothing, shoes (care and repair)	Allowances, grooming, personal expenses	Education, lessons, books, magazines, papers	Entertainment, recreation, gifts	Services	Other	TAX CONSIDERATIONS (Keep Receipts)				AVAILABLE CASH* (income, savings withdrawals, dividends and interest, bonuses, and loan proceeds)	
														Contributions	Medicines, prescription drugs	Dentist, doctor, medical, health insurance	Interest, taxes, child care, losses, professional and business expenses		
	Save	Life	House	Upkeep	Util.	Auto	Food	Cloth.	Pers.	Ed.	Fun	Serv.	Other	Give	Drugs	Doc.	Other	Source	Amount
Amount Budgeted																			
1																			
2																			
3																			
4																			
5																			
6																			
7																			
8																			
9																			
10																			
11																			
12																			
13																			
14																			
15																			
16																			
17																			
18																			
19																			
20																			
21																			
22																			
23																			
24																			
25																			
26																			
27																			
28																			
29																			
30																			
31																			
TOTALS																			

Total cash this month

MONTHLY SUMMARY

Last month's cash brought forward _____

This month's cash + _____

Total _____

Subtract total expenses this month – _____

BALANCE FORWARD

20

* Record income tax and retirement withholdings on income summary page 24.
Other payroll withholdings should be recorded in the appropriate columns on this monthly expense form.

MONTHLY EXPENSE CHART   MONTH _____ YEAR _____

	Operational savings, emergency savings, permanent savings	Life insurance	Rent or mortgage	Home upkeep, furnishings	Gas, lights, water, phone, trash, sewer	Transportation, auto upkeep, insurance	Food, sundries, paper and laundry products	Clothing, shoes (care and repair)	Allowances, grooming, personal expenses	Education, lessons, books, magazines, papers	Entertainment, recreation, gifts	Services	Other	TAX CONSIDERATIONS (Keep Receipts)				AVAILABLE CASH* (income, savings withdrawals, dividends and interest, bonuses, and loan proceeds)	
														Contributions	Medicines, prescription drugs	Dentist, doctor, medical, health insurance	Interest, taxes, child care, losses, professional and business expenses		
	Save	Life	House	Upkeep	Util.	Auto	Food	Cloth.	Pers.	Ed.	Fun	Serv.	Other	Give	Drugs	Doc.	Other	Source	Amount
Amount Budgeted																			
1																			
2																			
3																			
4																			
5																			
6																			
7																			
8																			
9																			
10																			
11																			
12																			
13																			
14																			
15																			
16																			
17																			Total cash this month
18																			
19																			
20																			
21																			MONTHLY SUMMARY
22																			
23																			Last month's cash brought forward _____
24																			
25																			This month's cash + _____
26																			
27																			Total _____
28																			Subtract total expenses this month − _____
29																			
30																			
31																			
TOTALS																			BALANCE FORWARD

Enter totals on summary page 27

* Record income tax and retirement withholdings on income summary page 24.
Other payroll withholdings should be recorded in the appropriate columns on this monthly expense form

MONTHLY EXPENSE CHART

MONTH _____ YEAR _____

| | Operational savings, emergency savings, permanent savings | Life insurance | Rent or mortgage | Home upkeep, furnishings | Gas, lights, water, phone, trash, sewer | Transportation, auto upkeep, insurance | Food, sundries, paper and laundry products | Clothing, shoes (care and repair) | Allowances, grooming, personal expenses | Education, lessons, books, magazines, papers | Entertainment, recreation, gifts | Services | Other | TAX CONSIDERATIONS (Keep Receipts) | | | | AVAILABLE CASH* (income, savings withdrawals, dividends and interest, bonuses, and loan proceeds) | |
| | | | | | | | | | | | | | | Contributions | Medicines, prescription drugs | Dentist, doctor, medical, health insurance | Interest, taxes, child care, losses, professional and business expenses | | |
	Save	Life	House	Upkeep	Util.	Auto	Food	Cloth.	Pers.	Ed.	Fun	Serv.	Other	Give	Drugs	Doc.	Other	Source	Amount
Amount Budgeted																			
1																			
2																			
3																			
4																			
5																			
6																			
7																			
8																			
9																			
10																			
11																			
12																			
13																			
14																			
15																			
16																			
17																			
18																			
19																			
20																			
21																			
22																			
23																			
24																			
25																			
26																			
27																			
28																			
29																			
30																			
31																			
TOTALS																			

Total cash this month

MONTHLY SUMMARY

Last month's cash brought forward _____

This month's cash + _____

Total _____

Subtract total expenses this month − _____

BALANCE FORWARD

22

Enter totals on summary page 27

* Record income tax and retirement withholdings on income summary page 24.
Other payroll withholdings should be recorded in the appropriate columns on this monthly expense form.

MONTHLY EXPENSE CHART

MONTH _____ YEAR _____

	Operational savings, emergency savings, permanent savings	Life insurance	Rent or mortgage	Home upkeep, furnishings	Gas, lights, water, phone, trash, sewer	Transportation, auto upkeep, insurance	Food, sundries, paper and laundry products	Clothing, shoes (care and repair)	Allowances, grooming, personal expenses	Education, lessons, books, magazines, papers	Entertainment, recreation, gifts	Services	Other	Contributions	Medicines, prescription drugs	Dentist, doctor, medical, health insurance	Interest, taxes, child care, losses, professional and business expenses	AVAILABLE CASH* (income, savings withdrawals, dividends and interest, bonuses, and loan proceeds)	
														TAX CONSIDERATIONS (Keep Receipts)					
	Save	Life	House	Upkeep	Util.	Auto	Food	Cloth.	Pers.	Ed.	Fun	Serv.	Other	Give	Drugs	Doc.	Other	Source	Amount
Amount Budgeted																			
1																			
2																			
3																			
4																			
5																			
6																			
7																			
8																			
9																			
10																			
11																			
12																			
13																			
14																			
15																			
16																			
17																			
18																			
19																			
20																			
21																			
22																			
23																			
24																			
25																			
26																			
27																			
28																			
29																			
30																			
31																			
TOTALS																			

Total cash this month [ ]

MONTHLY SUMMARY

Last month's cash brought forward _____

This month's cash + _____

Total _____

Subtract total expenses this month − _____

BALANCE FORWARD

* Record income tax and retirement withholdings on income summary page 24.
Other payroll withholdings should be recorded in the appropriate columns on this monthly expense form.

INCOME SUMMARY

Keep your paycheck stubs and record information on the Income Summary Form for two reasons: 1) to know where you stand and 2) to catch errors. Bosses and bookkeepers can and do occasionally make mistakes. When it is time to figure income taxes, you'll be glad to have this information all together. Keep paycheck stubs for proof until you receive W-2 or 1099 forms and then check your income totals against those reported to the government by your employer.

DATE	SOURCE	GROSS PAY (before withholdings)	Federal taxes	State taxes	Local taxes	FICA or retirement fund	OTHER AMOUNTS WITHHELD			NET PAY (after withholdings)

INCOME SUMMARY

DATE	SOURCE	GROSS PAY (before withholdings)	Federal taxes	State taxes	Local taxes	FICA or retirement fund	OTHER AMOUNTS WITHHELD			NET PAY (after withholdings)
TOTALS										

SAVINGS SUMMARY

TYPES OF SAVINGS: Keep each account separate such as emergency and savings accounts, credit unions, etc. On page 32, list IRA, Keogh, or other retirement funds.

	Name of savings institution				Name of savings institution				Name of savings institution				Other (CD's, savings bonds)
	Deposits	Withdrawals	Interest earned (quarterly)	Present balance	Deposits	Withdrawals	Interest earned (quarterly)	Present balance	Deposits	Withdrawals	Interest earned (quarterly)	Present balance	
JANUARY													
FEBRUARY													
MARCH													
APRIL													
MAY													
JUNE													
JULY													
AUGUST													
SEPTEMBER													
OCTOBER													
NOVEMBER													
DECEMBER													

SUMMARY OF YEARLY LIVING EXPENSES

	Life insurance	Rent or mortgage	Home upkeep, furnishings	Gas, lights, water, phone, trash, sewer	Transportation, auto upkeep, insurance	Food, sundries, paper and laundry products	Clothing, shoes (care and repair)	Allowances, grooming, personal expenses	Education, lessons, books, magazines, papers	Entertainment, recreation, gifts	Services	Other	Total living expenses (non tax deductible)
	Life	House	Upkeep	Utilities	Auto	Food	Clothing	Personal	Education	Fun	Services	Other	TOTALS
JANUARY													
FEBRUARY													
MARCH													
APRIL													
MAY													
JUNE													
JULY													
AUGUST													
SEPTEMBER													
OCTOBER													
NOVEMBER													
DECEMBER													
TOTALS													

SUMMARY OF MEDICAL DEDUCTIBLES

Keep this log as a health history even if you are not eligible for medical tax exemptions.

	Medicine			Doctors		Other: medical insurance premiums, hospital, dentures, glasses, rental medical equipment, physical therapy, mileage to doctor and hospital, etc.				ONE-TIME MEDICAL EXPENSES	
	Prescription	Amount	Miles Driven	Description	Amount	Description	Amount	Description	Amount	Description	Amount
JANUARY											
FEBRUARY											
MARCH											
APRIL											
MAY											
JUNE											
JULY											
AUGUST											
SEPTEMBER											
OCTOBER											
NOVEMBER											
DECEMBER											
	TOTAL		Total miles	TOTAL		TOTAL		TOTAL		TOTAL	

SUMMARY OF DEDUCTIBLE CONTRIBUTIONS

	CONTRIBUTIONS: Religious, service groups, business or professional expenses								One-Time Contributions	
	TYPE		TYPE		TYPE		TYPE		Description, To Whom	Amount
	Description	Amount	Description	Amount	Description	Amount	Description	Amount		
JANUARY										
FEBRUARY										
MARCH										
APRIL										
MAY										
JUNE										
JULY										
AUGUST										
SEPTEMBER										
OCTOBER										
NOVEMBER										
DECEMBER										
	TOTAL		TOTAL		TOTAL		TOTAL		TOTAL	

SUMMARY OF DEDUCTIBLE EXPENSES

INTEREST ON MORTGAGES AND OTHER LOANS, FINANCE CHARGES, CHARGE ACCOUNTS, AND CARRYING CHARGES
Interest on your home mortgage is wholly deductible at tax time. Even though other interest charges are no longer tax deductible, it is still very important to your financial picture to know how much interest you pay for the privilege of using someone else's money.

	House	Car payment						
JANUARY								
FEBRUARY								
MARCH								
APRIL								
MAY								
JUNE								
JULY								
AUGUST								
SEPTEMBER								
OCTOBER								
NOVEMBER								
DECEMBER								
TOTALS								

INSURANCE RECORDS

CAR, LIFE, HEALTH, THEFT, FIRE, PROPERTY, DISABILITY

Take a few minutes to fill in this chart for a visual overview of your insurance profile. Assess the adequacy of your coverage. Look at premium due dates. It may cause financial hardship if they all come due at the same time of year. Call agent to see about moving some due dates.

Policy number Name of company Name of agent	Date of purchase	Where document is located	Type of policy	Face Value	CASH VALUE (where applicable)		Enter in these columns exact date and amount due											
					This year	Upon death	Jan.	Feb.	Mar.	Apr.	May	June	July	Aug.	Sept.	Oct.	Nov.	Dec.

SUMMARY OF INVESTMENTS
REAL ESTATE, STOCKS, BONDS, CERTIFICATES AND OTHER ASSETS

Type and number	Indicate in whose name: husband, wife, or joint	Date acquired	Purchase price	Date sold	Sale price	Cost of sale	Amount gain or loss	Broker or agent	

SUMMARY OF INVESTMENTS

ITEMS WITH MATURITY DATES: CERTIFICATES OF DEPOSIT, MONEY-MARKET CERTIFICATES, REFUND AGREEMENTS,
MONEY FUNDS, AND ALL-SAVERS

Type and number	Date acquired	Purchase price	Percent interest rate	Number of months to term	Maturity date	Date cashed in	Name of financial institution where held	Indicate in whose name: husband, wife, child, or joint	Amount of gain

33

HOME MAINTENANCE AND CAPITAL IMPROVEMENTS

Home improvements, repairs, remodeling. Keep receipts indefinitely until last home is sold.

Date	Description of labor and materials	Amount

UTILITIES USAGE CHART

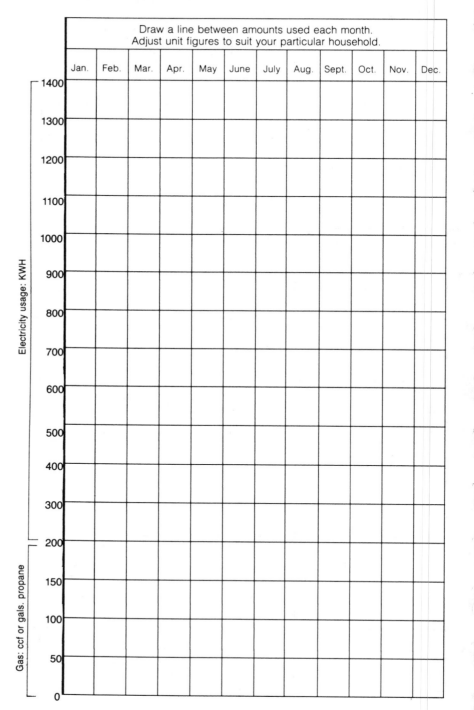

Draw a line between amounts used each month.
Adjust unit figures to suit your particular household.

Jan. Feb. Mar. Apr. May June July Aug. Sept. Oct. Nov. Dec.

Electricity usage: KWH

1400 1300 1200 1100 1000 900 800 700 600 500 400 300 200

Gas: ccf or gals. propane

150 100 50 0

AUTO MAINTENANCE

Date	Description of labor, parts, and who performed service	Mileage	Which car	Cost Labor	Parts	Date	Description of labor, parts, and who performed service	Mileage	Which car	Cost Labor	Parts

CREDIT CARDS

Take a moment to list all of your credit cards with their emergency phone numbers in case your wallet is lost or stolen.

COMPANY NAME	NUMBER	EXPIRATION DATE	CHARGE LIMIT	WHOM TO NOTIFY WHEN LOST OR STOLEN (see back of card for address)

HOUSEHOLD INVENTORY

Taking two hours to compile an inventory of your household belongings could be the cheapest form of property insurance you can invest in. It allows prompt, thorough and accurate filing of claims for natural calamity, and easy identification or proof of ownership in case of theft. It may also show a need for increased insurance. Starting at the front door and going clockwise around the house, write down the contents of each room. Fill in the appropriate headings for your rooms and storage areas, including the attic, basement and garage. If the item has a serial number or model number, use the next line in the form to record that number. Remember to include jewelry,

silver, china, crystal, works of art, stamp and coin collections, bicycles, valuable books and recordings, cameras, guns, fur coats, etc. Taking pictures of the rooms and your possessions could make identification or replacement easier. Arrange expensive collections such as silver and jewelry separately, and take close-up pictures. After compiling the inventory, make two more copies on a copy machine, send one to a reliable friend or insurance agent, and keep the other in your safe-deposit box.

LIVING ROOM			LIVING ROOM			KITCHEN			BEDROOM		
Item	Year bought	Cost	Item	Year bought	Cost	Item	Year bought	Cost	Item	Year bought	Cost

HOUSEHOLD INVENTORY

CLOTHES				Year bought	Cost		(room)			Year bought	Cost
Item	Year bought	Cost	Item			Item	Year bought	Cost	Item		

HOUSEHOLD INVENTORY

(room)			(room)			(room)			(room)		
Item	Year bought	Cost	Item	Year bought	Cost	Item	Year bought	Cost	Item	Year bought	Cost

IMPORTANT INFORMATION

ITEM	WHERE LOCATED	ITEM	WHERE LOCATED
Will		Income tax returns	
Lawyer's name		Family birth certificates	
Executor's name		Marriage certificate	
Power of attorney		Divorce papers	
Accountant's name		Driver's license numbers and expiration dates	
Insurance policies			
Insurance consultant		Car titles	
Safe deposit box number and key number			
Bank accounts and numbers		Car registration	
		Make: Model:	
Securities, stocks, bonds, certificates		Year: Vehicle I.D. #	
Real estate deeds		Family doctors	
Service serial number (dog tag)			
Social Security numbers		Medical records	
V.A. information		Immunizations	
Student numbers		Allergy and blood type	
Club membership numbers			

CUTTING FOOD COSTS

If you want to save money, stay out of stores. When you go, know what you want. Prepare a complete shopping list by making an inventory of your cupboards and refrigerator and by planning daily meals.

If you need to cut back, try working with the planning chart as shown. Estimate the cost of each item on your grocery list (see sample Breakfast and Lunch columns) and set mini-budgets. Add this up, rounding off as you go. If the total amount comes to more than your food allowance, you need to rework the menus and shopping list until it is within bounds.

It is less painful to go through this process at home than to overspend at the grocery store and then try to make it up in some other way. Even though food is a necessity, it needs a budget boundary. Preparing a shopping list and estimating costs before you step into the supermarket is one of those miracle strategies that pays off every time you use it.

Bulk items and staples

Amount budgeted: $ 48.00

Eggs	9.60
Milk	16.00
Oil	4.75
Flour	7.25
Peanut Butter	9.60

Laundry and paper product and toiletries

Amount budgeted: $ 45.00

detergent	15.60
shampoo	6.00
toilet paper	7.25
plastic bags	4.25
alum. foil	4.20
tissues	6.50

ESTIMATED FOOD BUDGET: $ 330.00 for 2 weeks
amount

BREAKFAST

Amount budgeted per shopping period $ 49.00

Amount budgeted per day $ 3.50

Menu	Need to buy	
orange juice	o.j.	9.00
oatmeal	blueberries	3.00
raisins	bread (3)	5.40
milk	jelly	3.50
Blueberry muff.	milk	7.75
juice		
soft-boiled eggs	apple juice	3.00
	cereal	12.50
toast		
juice		
cereal w/ fruit		
(etc.)		

LUNCH AND SNACKS

Amount budgeted per shopping period $ 37.00

Amount budgeted per day $ 2.60

Menu	Need to buy	
oatmeal cookies	tuna	5.50
cupcakes	crackers	4.25
popcorn	soup (4)	8.80
yoghurt	cheese	11.00
PB + J sands.	oranges	15.50
cheese sands.		
tuna salad sands.		
tom. soup w/ crackers		
egg salad sands.		
oranges		
school lunches	School	11.40
(etc.)		

DINNER

Amount budgeted per shopping period $ 144.20

Amount budgeted per day $ 10.30

Menu	Need to buy	
Main Dishes	Noodles	3.50
Spaghetti	Taco Shells	3.00
Tacos	Salmon	6.75
Chicken Teriyaki	Gr. Beef	17.00
Salmon	Buns	3.50
Hamburgers + beans (etc.)	Chicken III	15.00
	Pepperoni	4.75
Salads	Lettuce	3.50
Lettuce	Cabbage	1.85
carrot/pineapple	Tomatoes	5.50
cole slaw (etc.)	Carrots	3.50
	Gr. + red pepper	6.75
Vegetables (list each)	Raisins	4.75
	Celery	3.60
	Potatoes 10#	4.75
Desserts	Onions	2.50
(list each)	Broccoli	4.75
	(etc.)	

What to Keep and How To File It

Every home needs a system for the filing of personal records. No matter how modest your home facilities may be, you need a special place to keep tax records, legal items, insurance policies, and the like. The equipment you need does not have to be elaborate. A metal file cabinet is nice, but an accordian folder or a sturdy box with a lid will do just as well. The important thing is to keep everything together and organized—and to keep the system as simple as possible. It doesn't matter who organizes your home filing system, but use the talents of the person with the best business sense.

A simple subject file as shown is all most people need for their everyday papers. Irreplaceable papers should be kept in a safe-deposit box, vault, or safe. Do not keep will in safe-deposit box. Make photocopies to keep in your home files. Here are the important, hard-to-replace papers you should keep.

Safe Deposit Box

1. Birth Certificates
2. Citizenship Papers
3. Marriage Certificates
4. Adoption Papers
5. Divorce Decrees
6. Important Contracts but NOT Will
7. Death Certificates
8. Deeds
9. Titles to Automobiles
10. Household Inventory
11. Veteran's Papers
12. Bonds and Stock Certificates

After you have completed your tax return, put all the receipts, W-2 forms, checks that relate directly to entries on tax returns, records of interest payments, medical expenses, real estate taxes, and major expenses for sales tax into a large manila envelope along with a copy of your working tax return. This will help prevent a bad case of "nerves" should the IRS call you in for an audit. Keep the packet for seven years; save tax returns forever.

Remember to keep everything related to buying, selling, and improving a house—receipts, cancelled checks, and contracts—indefinitely until you sell your last home. If you have deferred the profit tax by re-investing your sales profit into another home, you will want to keep all of this information so that when you or your survivors finally make an accounting to the government, many of those expenses can be subtracted, decreasing the amount of taxable income.

Good money management also means good paper management.

GUARANTEES, WARRANTIES, AND SALES RECEIPTS FOR VALUABLE ITEMS

At my house, we found we needed more than one file folder to contain the instruction manuals and receipts for items under warranty. We purchased an expandable folder with alphabetical tabs and placed it in the financial file drawer because the sealed sides of the folder keep the smaller pieces of paper from getting lost. Sales receipts are stapled to accompanying data and filed under a logical topic (lawnmower is behind the letter L, blow dryer goes under B, etc.) We have to be on guard to capture that receipt or it will be misplaced or tossed out.

Basic principles of organization apply here because we had to first designate a place and second be very strict about getting the right papers to the right spot. Besides guarantees and proofs of purchase, we put operating instructions in the expandable file folder for all our appliances and machinery—lawn mower, hot-water heater, dishwasher, disposal. This is where you will find instructions for setting our various digital watches. We keep the serial numbers for the computer, vacuum, bicycles, and other equipment in this file. When something goes wrong with an item or it is stolen, we know where to look for any related information.

For the past five years, we have saved at least $300 each year on replacements and repairs by keeping track of these receipts and service orders. Just think how much income we would have to make before we had $300 to spend. Subtract taxes, FICA, and work-related expenses and you can see that we would have to earn almost $600 before we could go out and purchase those items again. Thus, to save money in this way is worth much more than gross income, and all it takes is a little time to get organized and self-control to keep track of those little pieces of paper.

The Wise Use of Credit

Instead of asking where your money has gone,
you should tell it where to go.

Are you managing your credit or is it managing you? Credit, the privilege of borrowing money, can be your servant or your master, depending on how wisely you use it. To begin with, your ability to borrow is determined by a "rating" issued by various credit reporting agencies. Your personal credit rating is established by a credit company which compiles information about your ability to repay, your character, the stability of your employment, your assets, and whether or not you have paid off previous loans. It is to your advantage to have good credit so you have an option to use it if you want.

Some people can handle credit cards and some can't. If you find yourself overbuying too often, or if you have trouble getting the accounts paid, or do not have a regular income, you may be better off not using them.

One reason some people have difficulty handling credit is that money looks like more BEFORE you get it than AFTER you get it. Suppose Jack is anticipating a tax refund of $1,200. For two months he considers all the hundreds of possible things he could buy with that hunk of money. If he starts making credit purchases before his windfall arrives, he will probably spend it more than once and end up in debt. Although the vision of "future money" magnifies its buying potential, writing down your plans will help focus the real image.

You need to take into account how much of your monthly or yearly income you will commit to credit purchases. "Planned debt" can be beneficial if you use sound reasoning and have the ability to repay. It can allow you to have the use of an item—such as a car, home, or equipment to start a business—before it is paid for. Credit can be like "reverse savings." It means getting the item first and then setting aside so much each month to pay for it, naturally, at a higher cost. Other people use credit as a budget, letting the bills tell them where all their money will have to go. Therefore, they are always spending their future money now.

Financial counselors suggest that no more than twenty percent of your take-home pay should go toward installment payments (not including home mortgage). Do you know how much of your income is going for things you purchase on credit? Very few people do, and very few realize how many dollars they are paying for interest. Take a minute right now, to figure roughly the percent of your take-home pay (after taxes and FICA or retirement) that is spent for credit purchases. If your total percentage (installment purchases and house payment) exceeds fifty percent, you may be heading for hard times.

List installment payments per month other than home mortgage:

Credit Card Accounts	_____
Car loans	_____
Recreational vehicle loans	_____
(boat, motorcycle, camper)	_____
Furniture	_____
_____	_____
_____	_____
Total Monthly Installment Payments	_____

Total Monthly Installment Payments ÷ Monthly Take-Home Pay = % of income going to installment payments (move decimal two places to right to get percentage)

_____   _____   _____

Example: Total Monthly Installment Payments = $460
Total Monthly Take-Home Pay = $1,600
.2875 = 28.75% (percent of income going to installment payments)
1,600 ⟌460

If you want to know the total percentage of your income going to repay debt, just add the house payment to the monthly installment payments and divide by the take-home pay:

Total Monthly Installment Payments + Monthly House Payment ÷ Monthly Take-Home Pay = % of income going to installment payments (move decimal two places to right to get percentage

_____   _____

Now that you know what percentage of your take-home pay you are spending for a house and other payments, you will be better able to judge when you can afford to take on more of those $10, $20, or $50 monthly debts.

If you are single and sharing apartment expenses, you can probably get by with spending a higher percentage of your income on credit purchases than if you had to worry about the fixed expenses of a home. It used to be said that the price of your home shouldn't be more than two and half times your gross annual income and that the payments shouldn't be over twenty-five percent of your gross monthly income. Very few people could buy a home under that rule anymore. Since house payments are taking staggering amounts of the family income, those who have a home and are paying more than twenty-five percent of their income for it cannot afford to spend another twenty percent of their income on installment payments and have anything left to live on.

There are no EASY payments, despite what you're led to believe by high-pressure salesmen, alluring displays, and enticing advertisements. Be wary of the small-amount-down and easy-payment or no-down-payment approach. It is always cheaper to buy with cash because buying on time involves carrying charges and interest. When you use credit, learn to use it wisely by (1) finding out exactly how much it is going to cost, (2) making as large a down payment as you can, and (3) taking the shortest time possible to pay back the balance. The larger the down payment and the shorter the repayment period, the lower the interest or finance charges will be.

You might consider freeing up some of your income by paying off some of your present installment payments. Suppose you are presently paying $600 a year *in interest* for installments. By putting off new purchases and concentrating on paying off existing loans, you could free up much of that money now going to payments and interest. Aren't there other things you would rather spend that $600 on? You can have as much as twenty percent more money to spend by postponing purchases and paying cash rather than paying "on time."

Some economists say, "borrow everything you can now and buy tangible items because the price will increase." The person who already has good control of his finances may beat inflation this way, but it is dangerous for most others. The problem is that the "hurry, spend now" theory nourishes a *habit*, develops a *lifestyle*, and creates the feeling that when a desire for something is felt, you should give in to that feeling and buy the item right now. The *emotional* feeling of having, getting, and possessing an item subsides quickly—long before the payments are finished. Then another desire begins to bud—the voice says, "buy now, before the cost goes up"— the payments overlap, and the debt gets bigger and bigger, because no matter what we have, we always want more. When the budget has reached its limits, the desire, though once satisfied, is active again. Yes, the item we bought last year would cost more if we had waited until this year, but the pleasure of newness is gone. By this time, if we try self-discipline and don't buy, we feel cheated, underappreciated, and depressed—causing other problems. If we buy (which is now an established spending pattern), even though we cannot afford it, we can get into serious financial trouble. It has been said that credit is the only way you can start at the bottom and go deeper in the hole. It is so easy to get trapped into thinking, "It's just $10 more a month," and not look at our total financial status. Because it is extremely expensive to use credit for making endless purchases, most people would be better off using credit cards only moderately, as a management tool rather than a loan instrument,

and easing away from the "hurry, buy now" theory in all forms of credit buying.

Before borrowing, ask yourself these questions:

1. Will the item for which I am borrowing still be usable after I have finished making the payments?
2. Have I read and do I understand everything in the contract? Are there any blank spaces? Do I get a copy of the contract?
3. Can I handle this added amount of debt without jeopardizing other commitments?
4. What will happen if I cannot make the payments? Will the item be repossessed? If it is repossessed, will I still owe the balance of payment? Will I also lose something else because I have signed it as collateral?
5. Are the guarantee, agreements, and promises in writing?
6. If married, have I discussed and agreed with my spouse on this matter?
7. Is this a planned, rather than an impulsive, purchase?
8. Would I buy this if I were paying cash?
9. Have I shopped to compare interest charges?

Borrowing on credit comes in many forms: credit card accounts, finance companies, banks, credit unions, and borrowing against a whole life insurance policy. The amount of money these companies charge for the use of their money can vary greatly. Charges for credit card accounts seem to be especially high, eighteen to twenty-two percent. You need to take into account these costs when you borrow, checking at least three different sources to compare the cost of the loan. The best way to compare the cost of credit from different sources is to ask for the "true" annual percentage rate of interest, which, according to the Federal Truth-in-Lending Law, must be shown to you as a percent and as the number of dollars. The following chart shows the amazing differences between the finance charges of various types of loan agencies. For instance, the charge for borrowing $3,000 for three years could run from $286 to $1,018. Although this chart shows estimates of the average rates several years ago, it may not reflect the actual interest rates today, because they change so quickly, but it shows the wide range of actual interest. It pays to shop around, especially for money.

Type of Credit	Range of Annual Percentage Rates	Average Annual Percentage Rate	Finance Charge (Based on Average Annual Percentage Rate)
Borrowing Against a Whole Life Insurance Policy	4-8%	6%	$286
Passbook Loan	7-12%	8½%	$410
Credit Union	9-12%	9½%	$460
Bank	10-15%	11%	$536
Car Dealer	12-16%	13½%	$665
Finance Company	18-23%	20%	$1,018

Chart put out by Bureau of Consumer Protection, booklet: **Credit Shopping Guide**

The annual percentage rates shown are estimates of national averages. The actual *annual percentage rate* is usually determined by law in your state, but some creditors charge less than the maximum.

If you are in trouble, there are places to go. Do not wait until you are in debt beyond your ability to repay. Since borrowing to consolidate your bills will only leave you with a bigger loan and longer time to pay, don't go to a loan company or finance company for advice. Hundreds of communities across the United States sponsor a consumer credit service and their help is FREE. Your city or state social service offices can tell you how to contact a consumer credit service, or write to Consumer Credit Counselling, 1275 K Street, Suite 885, Washington, D.C. 20005, for the address of the office nearest you. Most churches offer financial counseling as do banks, legal aid societies, credit unions, labor unions, and some company personnel departments. Service personnel can also get counseling from the Army or Navy. Very few of us learned enough economics in school or have had enough opportunity for practical experience to carry us through our entire life. We all need financial guidance once in a while.

There are often good reasons for borrowing, and credit can be used to your advantage if you plan carefully. By planning your debt, setting limits for the amount you will borrow, and comparing the cost of credit, you can keep your budget financially sound.

Family Cents

Your child's future happiness depends more on how he or she manages money than on how much he or she has.

For husband and wife, money management works best if it's on a partnership basis, with both parties having a voice in decision and policy making. When children become capable of understanding, they too should be involved in money concerns on a limited partnership basis.

As husband and wife, begin by discussing your money values together so that you understand each other. One partner may feel money is to spend, while the other feels it should be saved for the future. ALL couples will need to compromise to some degree when dealing with money because everyone has different expectations and wants. One of the trade-offs for love, security, and togetherness is that you cannot always have everything your way. Talking out your ideas will help in setting your goals together. A few people will find their ego is tied to spending: "If I can't have the best, I'm less than I want to be." Having something nice is important for all of us; but for some people, it is of prime importance. No one else can say what is right and wrong for a couple, but if a couple cannot come to some agreement and stick to their decisions, the money disagreements are likely to lead to other problems. This book is designed to help you understand each other's values a little better.

Besides dealing with each other's money values, there are two other important considerations that will help you in your money management as a couple:

1. Both partners need to be actively involved in family finance,

not only with the planning, but also with paying the bills. Even if one person is better at accounting, or if there is only one wage earner, taking a turn at paying the bills and balancing the accounts every few months will help each partner maintain a fresh view of their financial goals and problems. If one person handles the books exclusively, the other loses a true sense of where the money goes. Rotating this job also prepares both parties in case one should leave, die, or otherwise be unable to keep the books.

2. Both partners need personal allowances.

No matter how tight the budget, every individual needs some money for which he or she does not have to account to anyone. "Mad money," to spend on impulse or to save, makes a person feel like an important individual. When it is necessary to trim the budget, continuing the personal allowance makes it easier to cut down on other expenses, and having this allowance sets the limits each individual is free to spend as he chooses, safeguarding the money budgeted for other family needs. Although the allowance does not need to be accounted for, couples should be completely candid with each other in all other aspects of the budget.

Once the partners reach an understanding of their own money values, if there are children, then they are better able to strike a balance between family wants and needs. By involving the children in family finances, you help teach them to use money wisely. Because their happiness depends more on HOW they manage their money than on HOW MUCH they have, good money management skills are as important as career education. Here are five ways to help your children become better money managers.

1. Teach children to make money decisions within their capacities to comprehend.

If children do not have any money to spend, they cannot learn to manage it. As parents, you will want to see that they have *some* money, either as an allowance or earned. I have found that the allowance system, especially in the early years, seems to be more successful. I like to keep regular bedroom and household responsibilities as part of family membership, rather than related to money. An allowance, perhaps 50¢ per week per year of age (a seven-year-old would get $3.50 per week), gives a child enough money to experiment with for his needs and wants. That small amount certainly will not be all they need, but in the beginning it gives them enough to learn the value of various coins, how to make purchases, and then how to evaluate them. For instance, your son may decide to buy a little gadget that will break in a day. You might give advice, but not an ultimatum. The reason for having some money to spend is so the child can learn the consequences of making choices. When the flimsy little toy breaks, don't say, "I told you so," but help him evaluate what happened and consider possible alternatives next time.

2. Teach children early the importance of working and earning.

As a child grows, his needs and wants grow, creating the opportunity for him to earn money by working in addition to his regular family duties. This could be work that you might normally pay someone else to do around the home, or he can sell goods and services outside the family. This might include things like caring for the neighbor's yard or pets during vacations, babysitting, a paper route, or selling homemade bread. The challenge for parents is to carefully structure teaching situations and prepare their children for these working opportunities. Encourage them to take advantage of local training sessions such as classes on babysitting, first-aid, and proper care of equipment such as lawnmowers or bicycles.

It takes a little maturity to be able to wait a week or two for a paycheck. When young children first start to work for pay, they need immediate payoffs: sweep the porch now and receive a dime now. One mother went to the bank at the beginning of August and got $50 worth of coins and offered certain paying jobs (of course, after their regular chores and rooms were finished), to earn money for school supplies. Their mother may have bought the supplies anyway, but this opportunity taught a lesson about the value of money, and motivated the students to take better care of their school things. Just before school started, the children made two lists—one of wants and another of needs. Then they compared prices from the newspaper ads and went shopping. It was the highlight of the month.

3. Teach children to save.

Saving, a skill that goes along with money, must be done in small steps. You don't start by trying to get your child to put everything he receives into the bank for college (he doesn't even know what college is yet, although Mom and Dad may have started an account for him). First, he needs to learn to save with a goal in mind—something he wants and that he can afford to buy within a week or two. Later, he will be capable of saving a little longer for something.

My all time favorite success story about teaching children to save was told by a father who said he started to give his son an allowance when he was three. He began with 50 cents a week. The rule: he could spend half of it on anything he wanted, but the second half had to be put in his penny back until he had $10…at which time he could spend his savings on anything he wanted.

He spent his quarter every week on treats and trinkets; and dropped the other quarter in the bank, not hinking much about it. But when he reached his first $10 and realized what wonderful things he could get, he began saving all of his allowance so that he could have big things faster. Every year on his birthday, his allowance was increased. This child caught on to the rewarding concept of planned purchases versus the "spend every cent as you get it." Later, this boy was quite willing to open a long-term savings account.

Sometimes it works to match your child's savings effort for some items or expenses such as a bicycle. This will help the child adjust to realistic expectations—perhaps settling for a bike with fewer extras so he can have it sooner. Having to earn part of the cost himself frequently means he will take better care of it and helps the child purchase things beyond his financial abilities.

4. Teach children to manage their money.

Children need many varied experiences throughout their growing years to learn planning, evaluating, and decision making. A good time to do this is with clothing purchases. Suppose it is August and you have $100 to spend filling in the empty spots of a school wardrobe. This is not much money for clothes these days, but if the planning and buying are done together by the parent and child, the child is likely to be more satisfied with the clothing selections. He or she might take good care of the clothing and, perhaps, understand the trade-offs that have to be made when there is not enough money to buy everything new or now. These teaching opportunities can be structured to gradually give more and more responsibility to the child. One family has progressed to the point where the parents feel confident in giving each teen all his clothing and shoe allotment, school lunch money, bus fare, and allowance in one lump sum each month so he can do his own budgeting. Another lesson in budgeting might be to plan your family vacation together, discussing the total money allotted, how much will be needed for gas, food, and lodging, and how much will be left for fun and entertainment. You will not want to try all of these experiences at once, but one here and one there will eventually add up.

5. Involve children in decision making and goal setting.

As you set up and reevaluate your spending plan, let your children express their desires and feelings. Don and Jane Marcov used a visual experience to help their children understand the family budget. Don turned his paycheck in for cash, brought it home, and called everyone together for a family-council meeting. The kids' eyes widened as they saw that much real money, but registered disappointment as it went into each envelope for bills. They talked about getting a few of those dollars back by being more careful to close the outside doors, turn out lights, and take better care of what they already had. Another family tried to create the same type experience by using Monopoly money. Understanding the family financial plan and seeing it discussed openly will help children be able to choose a plan and handle their own affairs when they are adults. Older teens could also take a turn at balancing the family accounts and writing checks, although parents would have to sign them. You will probably need to mention that financial information is "private" and shared only within the family.

One final suggestion about money and the family: Without knowing it, you could be unfair in amounts spent on individual family members. Of course, each person has different needs because of age, sex, and position within the family, but you may be favoring one over the other without realizing it. Keep track for several months of the amount spent on each person of the family for clothes, shoes, recreation, etc. Sometimes it is a husband or wife who is overbuying for him or herself, or the parents might be neglecting their own needs to provide for the children.

Get the whole family into the money act. In the end, agreeing on goals and working toward them together will teach children about money and how to use it properly—which could yield a great amount of savings in more than just money.

Before You Spend . . .

To have what we want is riches,
but to be able to do without is power.

Shopping centers make most of their money from Friday night and weekend shoppers spending on impulse. (To spend on impulse means seeing and buying something you hadn't planned on buying.) These weekend spenders are telling themselves, "You work hard all week, you deserve a reward." And so they buy. Taking time to write down your financial goals, as suggested in the 8-Step Spending Plan, will help you make spending decisions with logic rather than emotion.

Every day, when I am working at my household tasks, I think of equipment or furnishings that would make work easier or things look nicer. I bet I could spend $200 a day. When I am working in the yard, it is poplar trees and tomato cages that I want; but at the same time, the workshop needs a power drill and sander. On cleaning day, I want a new vacuum. When we have company, I want a floor lamp and a side chair. This "I want-itis" can consume your whole life and make you unhappy. We need to learn to be satisfied with what we have and the rate at which we can accumulate. To help get control of these desires and whims, consider the following suggestions:

1. Stay out of stores.

If we were to go to the shopping mall today, we would find a bargain we truly needed. By staying home, we won't even know about it. Have you noticed that most rural families maintain a happy life without all the gadgets and conveniences that city homes have? They are not exposed to all the alluring array. They learn to live simply. If you look, you want; and finally, if you can't have it, you become dissatisfied and unhappy. If your favorite pastime is window-shopping, take up some other form of recreation.

2. Compare yourself to your ancestors.

Did they need it? What quality of life did they have without it? I don't want to go back to outhouses and cold water, but it is possible to live a good life without an electric can opener or a massage shower head. Poverty can be a state of mind, rather than a situation. We need not deprive ourselves of everything, but we do need to get control of how we spend. Continue asking yourself these questions before you buy.

3. Ask yourself, Is this item important to my future?

Sunglasses? CD player? If it isn't essential, perhaps you can wait a little longer. You need to ask yourself many questions to get control of the "I want-itis" disease. How much of my life, work, and time is this item worth? Several years ago, I wanted a dehydrator for drying fruits and vegetables. I looked over all the models. I planned and calculated but just couldn't come up with the $150. The only possible way to get it was to take on some outside work. My time was already completely obligated with family, including a nine-month-old baby. When I evaluated what part of my life I would have to give up for a dehydrator, I decided to do without.

4. Keep an "I-want list."

When money is available, you can choose from the list what you want most, not just what you happen to want today, or what you see now. Writing it down frees your mind, but keeps the thought. Start a "want list" for each member of the family and one for the house. Keep these lists in one place, perhaps in the back of this budget book or in a planning notebook. When a child comes to you with a "want," let him see you write it on his list, and he will know you take his feelings seriously. These "want lists" will give clues for birthday or holiday giving and can really be fun. For example, if a child is shopping with me, and I notice things she is longing for, I jot them down on her want list. Appropriate clothing sizes are also kept on this list. Having these ideas written down can help you plan your buying, give time to watch for sales, and save hours of shopping time.

5. Consider how much it will cost to maintain it.

(Both time and money.) One family realized their dream of a swimming pool, but were unprepared for the huge heating bills, the price of a fence for protection and privacy, or the many hours required for daily cleaning. What is your time worth? Many people today won't buy anything but wash and wear clothes and linens because they hate to spend time ironing. Everything has its care price. A new end table is one more thing to dust and polish. A plant needs watering, feeding, spading, and a monthly shower. We continue taking more into our lives, each requiring a few more dollars and a few more moments, until we are slaves to our belongings. Does the pleasure of owning this item outweigh its "care" price? As a final test, you might ask yourself, "how well do I take care of what I have?"

6. Ask yourself, How long will this be useful to me?

What's desirable to you today may not be desirable in four years. To get control of your spending, continue asking yourself, "Where will I put it" If you answer, "Oh, but I want it so much, I will find a place for it," watch out; that philosophy will overfill the house. Do you use what you have? How often have you really wanted something, then when you got it, found you didn't use it? Do you use the slow cooker and cookie shooter? Will this be just another "shelf hog"?

Ask yourself, "What else can I use or do instead?" After accepting that I could not afford a dehydrator, I went to a demonstration on food drying and learned it could be done in the oven. My husband and I spent an hour making four screen racks for the oven. That season we dried every fruit and vegetable we could and found we did not care for dried vegetables. In the end, I didn't need the dehydrator.

7. Be inventive.

Whenever we want something, our first impulse is to go get it (that's why when we do so, it is called impulse buying). Many times something else will do just as well if we stop and use our imaginations. One day when I didn't have time to iron the linen tablecloth, I wanted to go buy a new no-iron cloth, but it was the end of the month and there was no money. Instead, I tried using a large piece of polyester knit from my sewing closet. It worked so well and cost so little that the linen cloth is still in the inactive storage. Our neighbor used clamp-on ice shoes he bought for 50¢ at a garage sale to aerate his lawn. You can be imaginative; give it a try.

8. Set money limits before going shopping.

A gift is only a token. Forget the idea that the monetary value of a gift has to equal the depth of your love, and you won't be tempted to buy something on impulse that costs too much. Avoid impulsive buying and overspending by setting a limit, planning, and comparing. Keep a general merchandise catalogue, such as those from Wards or Sears, to get a general idea of a particular item's price before you start looking. Sometimes catalogue prices are the best buy if you don't have to pay much for shipping. If you do comparison shopping, you will know a good bargain when you see it. Since you can't have everything, choose what you can have with care.

9. Do it yourself.

Ben Franklin said, "A penny saved is a penny earned." Suppose you can fix your own washing machine for which the bill would have been $125. To hand out that much spendable income a worker might have had to earn $227 gross salary (it is not unusual for a worker to lose half his salary to withholdings). We can't do everything ourselves, but nowadays, it literally can pay to be handy. At the time of purchase for a major appliance, go straight to the service department and order a service manual. Then, when something goes wrong, you can make a reasonable evaluation of what the trouble is and whether fixing it is within your mechanical abilities as a novice, or whether you would be better off hiring a professional or just buying a new one. It might pay to specialize in a service so you can trade labor with friends. Books that tell how to service small and major appliances (everything from a heating pad to the clothes dryer) are available to borrow from your local library or to buy at book or hardware stores.

One time, a woman said to me, "We have been married just about the same number of years, have the same income, same number of children—why is it that you always seem to have more money to spend for the fun little things?" As we traced back our spending patterns, we found two major reasons for my family to have $170 to $300 a month more to play with than they: (1) Because they insisted on having new cars when they bought, their monthly car payments were usually $160 more than ours, and (2) they paid someone else to do all the home and auto maintenance and repair work—not even changing their own oil and filters. These two lifestyle patterns alone made quite a dollar difference. This is where personal values come in, and these choices need to be made with your desires and abilities in mind.

10. Take care of things.

Oiling, painting, and cleaning at the right time will make things last longer. If you can make your lawnmower last two years longer by keeping it out of the rain and taking proper care of the motor, it is to your financial advantage. Cleaning the dried leaves out of the roof gutters and patching the leaks before the spring rains may save not only money, but also time cleaning up the mess later from a flood.

Have fun with your money, but before you spend, PLAN. Planning means writing it down and the word for that is BUDGET. A budget is not a one-shot deal, something you make once and never touch again. Instead you keep reworking a budget until it works for you and the results satisfy you. This means making, evaluating, revising, and remaking. Eventually, you may get to the point where it isn't necessary to write down all the facts and figures; your checkbook stubs may be enough unless you make a special purchase or set a special goal. As things change, reorganize your goals around your new life style and make a new list of goals.

After you have planned HOW to spend your money, use self-discipline and carefully consider your decisions before spending. The plan will not work unless you DO IT.

Dollar Stretching Tips

The real trouble with money is

you can't use it more than once.

The following pages offer tips for stretching the dollar. No one will use all of them, because our lifestyles are so different. For myself, besides trying to apply the ten suggestions to control buying, I have found that the best way to save money is to *stay out of stores!* Find some other source of recreation. When my family was little, I made my own bread and we drank powdered milk, cutting out the biweekly grocery store stops. I bought meat, eggs, cheese, baking staples, and grains in quantity (we have our own flour mill); preserved fruits, vegetables, and nuts in their season; and grew a garden to stay away from stores.

For me, the second best way to save money and stretch the dollar is to *plan* and then buy at seasonal sales. We spend less than half what the average U.S. family spends on clothing because I mend clothing promptly and sew some of our clothing (also buying fabric and notions at seasonal sales—New Year's Day is my favorite). The things that I do not make, we plan and buy at the right time. For instance, because shoes go on sale after Christmas, before Easter, and before school starts in September, we try to buy at thos times. But remember, when an item is on sale, even at half price, you do not save anything if you buy more than you need. The emotional thrill of a bargain can actually cause you to overbuy—so beware!

As you read through the following lists, check off the ideas you would like to try. First start shaving on the biggest expenditures, working down to the smallest expenses. For example, you could cut down on the hundreds of dollars that the average American spends on clothing every year by sewing some of your own, even though the use of a machine actually increases the utility bill. Why go to bed at sunset to save pennies on your utility bill when caulking around the windows could save many more dollars? It costs $1.60 to use a 100-watt bulb for ten hours. Heating and cooling offer your best opportunity to save energy money because they are the larger portion of the utility bill. Start by trying to save on the biggest expenses first.

GENERAL SAVING TIPS

- [ ] Stay out of stores as much as possible, even just to look.
- [ ] Watch the cash register as the items are rung up; look over the sales slip; count your change.
- [ ] Check the quality; read labels; examine products for workmanship.
- [ ] Don't be afraid to ask the price.
- [ ] Buy in quantity if you will use it and have a place to store it.
- [ ] Shop for true bargains at seasonal sales, factory outlets, and no-frill stores.
- [ ] Form a co-op and get group prices.
- [ ] Take advantage of rebates.
- [ ] Pay bills on time to save finance charges.
- [ ] In some states you can get a sales tax license and buy wholesale.
- [ ] Pay cash to save interest and service charges.
- [ ] Shop in the yellow pages.
- [ ] Buy at the source where items are made or grown.
- [ ] Plan ahead to anticipate future purchases.
- [ ] Buy only when relaxed—you will not make as many mistakes.
- [ ] Avoid impulse buying of things you did not plan on.
- [ ] Take TIME to decide.
- [ ] Use the phone to make sure the store or office is open, that they have what you want, and to compare costs.
- [ ] Get a written estimate before hiring someone to build, repair, etc.
- [ ] Before buying, consult with friends who have had experience with the product.
- [ ] Keep a general merchandise catalogue like the ones from Wards or Sears for price comparison.
- [ ] Look at consumer report magazines or in yearly buying guides for ratings.
- [ ] Don't buy from vending machines, which charge more for stamps, pop, candy, and cigarettes.
- [ ] Watch for shipping or handling charges.
- [ ] Compare local and national brands.
- [ ] Consider buying at discount stores or in low-rent areas where prices may be lower.
- [ ] Take care of what you buy.
- [ ] Read the instructions and DO what they say.
- [ ] Wash, clean, and oil at the right times.
- [ ] Keep guarantees and sales receipts in case an item needs repair or replacement.
- [ ] Do it yourself. (Call your county agent for advice or use your local library.)
- [ ] Send for consumer information from the government (see page 58) and local agencies.

- ☐ Watch for how-to books; they cover everything from mending your own shoes to making cleaning solutions.
- ☐ Buy basic repair manuals to learn how to make simple home repairs yourself.
- ☐ Trade services. If you don't already have a skill, learn one. "I will help you build a fence if you will help me put in a sprinkling system." Or, "I will decorate a birthday cake for you if you will give me a permanent."

CLOTHING

- ☐ Plan your wardrobe and buy clothes that can be worn for many occasions.
- ☐ Buy the simple classic clothing styles rather than the high fashion versions.
- ☐ Establish a basic color theme for your wardrobe.
- ☐ Make a list of the clothes you have and what you use them for. Sell or give away those clothes you haven't worn in the last year.
- ☐ Make a priority list of items you need and want.
- ☐ Shop for minor clothing and accessories that will expand your present wardrobe.
- ☐ Purchase wisely; buy only clothes that fit properly; try them on.
- ☐ Read the content label to evaluate costs for dry cleaning or special care.
- ☐ Look for good workmanship. Inspect seams, grain of fabric, hems, buttons, linings, and zippers. (True value is seldom measured by price alone.)
- ☐ Set a monthly clothing budget and *stick to it!*
- ☐ Find a dressmaker who can do a good job on necessary alterations and repairs.
- ☐ Follow ads carefully to determine what kind of merchandise is on sale.
- ☐ Take advantage of clearances, closeouts, and inventory reductions.
- ☐ Do not overbuy just because something is on sale.
- ☐ Consider irregulars or factory outlets.
- ☐ Never buy a whole new wardrobe all at once. It will wear out or you will get tired of it all at once.
- ☐ Watch for what you need at "near new" shops, Salvation Army clothing stores, garage sales, rummage sales, and auctions.
- ☐ Most pattern companies feature easy-to-sew items. Look into these for summer clothes, children's clothes, tablecloths, curtains, etc.
- ☐ Buy fabric, patterns, and notions at seasonal sales.
- ☐ Knit your own sweaters, scarves, and hats.
- ☐ Recycle what you can.
- ☐ Mend clothes promptly so you don't lose the whole garment.
- ☐ Treat spots and stains immediately.
- ☐ Choose correct water temperature and washing cycle to avoid setting stains, fading, or shrinking.
- ☐ Treat soiled clothing with care. Do not let it be thrown on the floor or get walked on.
- ☐ To avoid mildew, air-dry all garments before rehanging in closet or putting into hamper.
- ☐ Keep clothes out of direct sunlight.
- ☐ Hang heavier garments on wooden or thick plastic hangers to limit stretching and sagging.
- ☐ Button and zip garment after it is on hanger.
- ☐ Wash or dry clean clothing before storing for a season.
- ☐ Use moth protection when storing woolens.
- ☐ Use self-service dry cleaning for items (like sweaters) that do not have to be professionally pressed.
- ☐ Change from expensive clothing to casual clothes upon arriving home.
- ☐ Use aprons, bibs, coveralls, or smock tops when appropriate.
- ☐ Throw out rusty hangers before they stain your clothing.

SHOES

- ☐ Buy during seasonal sales—especially after Christmas, before Easter, and before school starts in September.
- ☐ Look for well-made shoes that can be repaired.
- ☐ Always try on shoes for proper fit.
- ☐ Buy shoes that can be worn on many occasions and with more than one outfit.
- ☐ Air shoes to give perspiration a chance to evaporate.
- ☐ Alternate between two pairs of shoes.
- ☐ Polish leather shoes regularly.
- ☐ Insert shoe trees when storing shoes.
- ☐ Use shoe horn to put on shoes.
- ☐ If your shoes get wet, stuff them with old towels or absorbent rags and let them dry away from direct heat. Polish or rub lightly with mineral oil when dry.
- ☐ Waterproof your boots and shoes *before* it rains. (Waterproofing is inexpensive compared to the cost of new shoes.)
- ☐ Wear overshoes in bad weather.

FOOD

- ☐ Plan menus before you shop.
- ☐ Determine food budget limits before shopping.
- ☐ Prepare a list *before* shopping, considering seasonal products, specials, and your needs.
- ☐ Figure the cost per serving or cost per meal to see where the money really goes.
- ☐ Go shopping only *once* during each pay period.
- ☐ Buy only what's on your list; avoid all impulse buying.
- ☐ Don't go shopping when you are sick, hungry, depressed, or angry.
- ☐ Market early or late to avoid crowds.
- ☐ Leave children and spouse at home.
- ☐ Use the "unit pricing" information that most stores provide.
- ☐ Try buying store brand products or generic items.
- ☐ Take advantage of items on the day-old-baked-goods rack. Freeze and heat later in oven to perk up flavor.
- ☐ If you decide to buy an unplanned special, eliminate another item of equal value from your list.
- ☐ Compare frozen, fresh, and canned fruits and vegetables for best value. Sliced or cut foods often cost less than whole foods.
- ☐ Check newspapers and magazines for coupons for items you normally buy.
- ☐ Ask local grocery store to set aside a corner for a "coupon exchange" box.
- ☐ If a store runs out of a special you want, ask for a raincheck.
- ☐ Drink water at meals and cut down on sweet drinks and pop.
- ☐ Cut down or eliminate potato chips and other crunchy, salty snacks.
- ☐ Try powdered milk for cooking or drinking.
- ☐ Eat less meat (especially red meat). Use extenders and protein complements to insure full protein nutrition.
- ☐ When buying meat, consider the cost per serving rather than cost per pound.
- ☐ Buy whole chickens, meat, and cheese. Cut and wrap for your needs.
- ☐ Roast your own cold cuts.
- ☐ Do not buy bacon.
- ☐ If you go hunting or fishing, use the game meat.
- ☐ Avoid convenience and highly processed foods.
- ☐ Put together your own mixes to make cakes, pancakes, and cookies.
- ☐ Grow a garden! (Cheapest way to get fresh foods.)

- [ ] Take lunch from home.
- [ ] Make desserts, bread, rolls, stuffing, and croutons at home.
- [ ] Chop your own nuts.
- [ ] Make your own syrups and jellies—very easy!
- [ ] Serve hot cereals for breakfast instead of high-cost dry cereals.
- [ ] Use leftovers. Freeze gravy, vegetables, and meat for "end-of-the-month soup."
- [ ] Keep basic baking staples on hand so you can make a variety of things without returning to the store.
- [ ] Buy and maintain a freezer for fewer shopping trips.
- [ ] Shop at a co-op or warehouse, or join a buying club.
- [ ] Buy food from farm stands or farmers's markets. (Check newspaper want ads.)
- [ ] Take your own food with you on drives, to the movies, on picnics.
- [ ] When you're on vacation, try buying one meal per day at a grocery store rather than a restaurant. (Yogurt and bananas are great for breakfast or lunch!)
- [ ] Have several frozen or quick meals on hand so you won't be tempted to go out to eat when it is too late to start dinner or you are tired.

HOME

- [ ] Maintain your home by cleaning spots immediately.
- [ ] Check furnace, hot water heater, and air conditioner regularly; lubricate where necessary and change filters.
- [ ] Inspect gutters, concrete, trim, and siding for trouble and do regular maintenance to minimize large repairs or replacement costs.
- [ ] Do your own painting and wallpapering. (Invite a friend to help.)
- [ ] In your yard and garden, plant native varieties of trees and shrubs—they require less care than exotic hybrids.
- [ ] Mulch around flowers, trees, shrubs, and in garden to hold water in soil.
- [ ] To save watering and maintenance, put rocks in part of the yard.
- [ ] Sprinkling systems use less water than sprinklers which must be manually moved.
- [ ] Consider drip irrigation where watering is restricted or expensive.
- [ ] Buy fertilizer by cubic yard rather than in 50-pound bags if you use very much.
- [ ] Rent rather than buy tools and equipment, especially if only needed occasionally.
- [ ] Share cost of major purchases like rototiller, snowblower, lawnmower, and large ladder.
- [ ] Start your own flowers and vegetables from seed rather than buying them ready-to-plant.
- [ ] Check the possibility of buying plants from agricultural colleges, nurseries, and occupational technical centers.

FURNITURE

- [ ] Rent instead of buy.
- [ ] Buy it used.
- [ ] Make a decision on the type or style furniture you want.
- [ ] Know how many pieces you need and where they will go.
- [ ] Make sure that the style will be continued if you do not buy the complete set now.
- [ ] Buy furniture with a variety of uses, perhaps to be used in more than one room.
- [ ] Buy antiques if you want your furniture to increase in value.
- [ ] Classic furniture styles will not be outdated as quickly as modern styles.
- [ ] Measure your rooms before buying furniture.
- [ ] Make a scale model of each room on graph paper.
- [ ] Measure your areas and the furniture before buying—include height, depth, and width.

- [ ] Measure entranceways to be sure furniture will fit.
- [ ] Take color samples with you.
- [ ] Check for quality.
- [ ] Consider the following: How can it be cleaned? Will it fade? Will it snag? Will it split? Can it be repaired in case of burns or tears? Will this fabric wear well? Are patterns or stripes matched?
- [ ] Look for a design that can be re-covered or re-upholstered.
- [ ] Read Consumer Reports on comparative price and quality.
- [ ] Send for free government information.
- [ ] Re-upholster cloth furniture yourself.
- [ ] Make or buy fabric furniture covers.
- [ ] Buy unfinished furniture and paint it yourself.
- [ ] Touch up or refinish old furniture.
- [ ] Scotch Guard everything.
- [ ] Clean furniture regularly.
- [ ] Vacuum upholstered furniture and drapes at least once every two months.
- [ ] Polish wood furniture at least once a month.

APPLIANCES

- [ ] Buy dual-purpose items when possible (such as combination mixer and blender).
- [ ] Consider no-frill models.
- [ ] Last year's model, even new, may cost less than this year's model.
- [ ] Look in newspapers and on bulletin boards for used items.
- [ ] Buy demonstrators or appliances used by schools. Ask the school which dealer to check with for details.
- [ ] Determine if your space is wide enough and tall enough for the appliance.
- [ ] Don't buy any appliance in a size larger than you need (hot water heater, washing machine, etc.).
- [ ] Consider the availability of service.
- [ ] Is there a guarantee or warranty?
- [ ] Can you use other than factory-approved outlets for repair?
- [ ] Does the price include: Parts? Freight? Installation? Removal of old appliance? Labor? House-call charge? Follow-up?
- [ ] For maintenance, read instruction books carefully and follow their advice.
- [ ] Keep operating, installation, and service instructions in one place.
- [ ] Oil and clean appliances regularly.
- [ ] Watch for burned out fuses and cords with loose wires.
- [ ] Consider ordering a service repair manual when purchasing a new major appliance; don't wait until you need it.
- [ ] Compare energy costs before buying special features (for example, compare energy costs of a frost-free versus manual defrost refrigerator, electric ice maker versus plastic ice cube trays).
- [ ] Compare water consumption costs for shower heads, washing machines, and dishwashers.
- [ ] Do not leave your appliances running when they are not in use.
- [ ] Empty or replace the vacuum cleaner bag frequently.
- [ ] Locate your refrigerator and freezer away from heat sources.
- [ ] Do not keep your refrigerator or freezer too cold.
- [ ] Never allow frost to build up more than one-quarter of an inch because it acts as an insulator rather than a coolant.
- [ ] Vacuum the grills and evaporation coils to remove accumulated dust every three months.
- [ ] Do not put warm foods directly into the refrigerator or freezer.

- ☐ Cover all foods to prevent evaporation and to save your cooling unit extra work.
- ☐ Check the tightness of your refrigerator door gasket by shutting a dollar bill in the door. If the bill slides out without resistance, your refrigerator may be leaking cold air, meaning the gasket needs to be readjusted or replaced—or the door tightened.
- ☐ Open doors only when necessary and close them as soon as possible.
- ☐ In the laundry, use water no hotter than necessary for adequate soil removal and sanitation.
- ☐ Use variable water levels for smaller batches of washing.
- ☐ Use the suds saver if you have one.
- ☐ Pre-soak or use a soak cycle when washing soiled garments.
- ☐ Wash only full loads of laundry.
- ☐ Rinse with cool water.
- ☐ Keep lint screen in dryer clean.
- ☐ Fill clothes dryer but do not overload it.
- ☐ Keep the outside exhaust clean.
- ☐ If your dryer has an automatic dry cycle, use it. Overdrying merely wastes energy and wears out the clothing.
- ☐ Separate drying loads into heavy and lightweight items, since the lighter items require less drying time.
- ☐ Save energy by using the old-fashioned clothesline.
- ☐ To save money on water bills, take showers rather than tub baths.
- ☐ Install a flow restrictor in the pipe at the showerhead to reduce the flow of water per minute.
- ☐ Promptly repair leaky faucets.
- ☐ Do as much household cleaning as possible with cold water.
- ☐ Clean up spills and countertops with sponge or dishcloth rather than expensive paper towels.
- ☐ Insulate your hot water storage tank and piping, especially if they run through a cold basement.
- ☐ Check the temperature of your water heater. Most water heaters are set for 140° F or higher, but you may not need water that hot.
- ☐ Drain out sediment in the bottom of the hot water heater by drawing out several gallons of water from the tank through the drain faucet at the bottom.
- ☐ To save money in the kitchen, use a sink stopper or dish pan rather than washing and rinsing dishes under running hot water.
- ☐ Be sure your dishwasher is full, but not overloaded, when you turn it on. (The average dishwasher uses 14 gallons of hot water per load.)
- ☐ When buying a dishwasher, look for a model with air-power and/or overnight dry settings.
- ☐ Let your dishes air-dry. If you do not have an automatic air-dry switch, turn off the control knob after the final rinse, prop the door open a little, and air-dry the dishes.
- ☐ Scrape dishes before loading them in the dishwasher for cleaning efficiency and fewer repair costs.
- ☐ Use cold water rather than hot to operate your food disposal.
- ☐ Install an aerator in your kitchen sink faucet.
- ☐ If you have a gas stove, make sure the pilot light is burning efficiently. (A yellowish rather than a blue flame means you're burning fuel inefficiently.)
- ☐ Keep lids on pans for best use of heat. Do not even boil water in an open pan.
- ☐ Keep range-top burners and reflectors clean.
- ☐ Thaw foods before cooking.
- ☐ Match the size of the pan to the heating element. Flat-bottomed pans receive heat directly and conserve energy.
- ☐ If you cook with electricity, get in the habit of turning off the burners several minutes before the allotted cooking time.
- ☐ Make the most of oven heat by cooking several things at the same time.
- ☐ In the oven, glass and ceramic dishes transfer heat better than metal, meaning you can lower the temperature 25 degrees.
- ☐ Do not continually open the oven door to check food; use a clock or use a timer or look through the window.
- ☐ For small meals, use small electric pans or ovens.
- ☐ Use pressure cookers and microwave ovens if you have them.
- ☐ When cooking with a gas range-top burner, use moderate flame settings to conserve gas. (The flame should never extend beyond the bottom of the pan.)
- ☐ Choose to use the range top rather than the oven when you have a choice.

RECREATION AND ENTERTAINMENT

- ☐ Buy season tickets rather than individual tickets to concerts, plays, or games.
- ☐ Go to little league ball games or high school games.
- ☐ Take in the dollar movies or a drive-in.
- ☐ Take your own treats or refreshments when you go.
- ☐ Use promotion coupons from local newspapers when eating out.
- ☐ Have cocktails at home *before* you go to a restaurant.
- ☐ Invite people in to share an evening rather than going out.
- ☐ Ask others to help bring food and drinks.
- ☐ Picnic by the fireplace—roast hot dogs and marshmallows.
- ☐ Have a surprise dinner—everyone gets $5 to buy something, whatever he chooses.
- ☐ Plan a progressive dinner with friends.
- ☐ Borrow a movie from the library, pop some corn, and show the film after dark on the patio for your own outdoor theater.
- ☐ Subscribe to your favorite magazines rather than buy them off the rack.
- ☐ Borrow books, magazines, records, and movies from a library or friend.
- ☐ Trade the books you have read for credit toward purchase at used book stores.
- ☐ Take a sightseeing tour of your city.
- ☐ Watch trains, planes, boats, people.
- ☐ Watch for FREE community concerts in the park, art exhibits, lectures, classes, films, story hours, and demonstrations.
- ☐ Check newspapers, bulletin boards, posters.
- ☐ Look through the yellow pages.
- ☐ Check library handouts.
- ☐ Write to your local Chamber of Commerce.
- ☐ Contact your local YMCA and community center for list of their activities.
- ☐ Ask your friends what they do for fun.
- ☐ Take a tour of a farm, newspaper, industry, TV station, radio station, bakery, cookie factory, auto plant, mining operation, brewery, movie studio, dairy, cannery, recording studio.
- ☐ Take advantage of events sponsored by local churches, schools, and universities: bazaars, carnivals, flea markets, recitals, ball games, dances, movies, and fund-raising food projects.

TELEPHONE

- ☐ If your phone bill has been paid on time for over a year, call and ask for a return of your deposit—they will send it with interest.
- ☐ To avoid paying a deposit, provide letter from person or firm with established good credit saying that they will be responsible for any of your charges not paid.

- [ ] Examine your monthly bill for possible mistakes or unnecessary services.
- [ ] If you reach a wrong number when making a long-distance call, call the operator immediately and report it. You will not be charged for the call.
- [ ] When you call for directory assistance, jot down the number and save it to avoid another charge.
- [ ] Make long-distance calls when discount rates are in effect. (It costs more to make a call Sunday evening than Sunday morning.)
- [ ] Dial your own long-distance calls.
- [ ] Talk less—plan your calls before placing them. (Try setting a timer.)
- [ ] Did you know you can send a letter special delivery for less than the average long-distance phone call?
- [ ] Tape your message on a cassette recorder (just pretend you are talking on the phone, but you haven't given them a chance to answer yet), then mail it. You are not obligated to fill up the whole tape.

ON THE ROAD

- [ ] Share your rides with friends.
- [ ] Go shopping with a neighbor occasionally.
- [ ] Don't overfill your tank.
- [ ] Do not let the motor idle for more than a minute.
- [ ] Minimize braking.
- [ ] Drive at a smooth and steady pace.
- [ ] Accelerate smoothly—rapid acceleration and sliding stops eat away tires and gas.
- [ ] Observe speed limits.
- [ ] If heating or cooling your car is necessary, use a moderate setting.
- [ ] Studies show an air conditioner costs less to run than the money lost in increased gas consumption due to air friction from open windows at highway speeds.
- [ ] Remove unnecessary weight from the car—an extra 100 pounds decreases fuel economy about one percent.
- [ ] Keep track of gas mileage for clue that something is wrong.
- [ ] Don't drive, if you can get there on public transportation.
- [ ] Take advantage of monthly discounts on tickets or tokens.
- [ ] Walk to work or school—it takes less time than you think and makes you feel great when you get there!
- [ ] Ride a bike.
- [ ] Eliminate trips by preplanning.
- [ ] Call ahead to make sure stores or offices are open.
- [ ] Do not have a car, especially a second car, unless you have to.
- [ ] Vacation near home.
- [ ] Buy the most fuel-efficient car of the size and style you want. Price could be a factor.
- [ ] Purchase only the optional equipment and accessories you really need.
- [ ] When buying a new car, research both government buying guides and commercial buying guides.
- [ ] Go for a test drive.
- [ ] Compare fuel economies.
- [ ] Consult road tests.
- [ ] Shop around for the best financing.
- [ ] Compare prices with at least three dealers.
- [ ] Read the owner's manual *before* you buy.

- [ ] Give a great deal of consideration to service and the availability of parts.
- [ ] *Before* buying, determine whether service department is conveniently located.
- [ ] Sit in all seats, including the back, to evaluate comfort, leg and head room.
- [ ] Carefully figure how much is being credited for a trade-in. Sometimes the cost is less if you pay cash.
- [ ] Understand exactly what accessories are included in the price.
- [ ] Make sure you fully understand the warranty.
- [ ] Is it a full warranty including parts AND labor, or is it a limited warranty?
- [ ] Read the requirements for all warranties.
- [ ] On delivery, check carefully to see that the car is delivered as ordered—including all accessories. Once you drive the car off the lot, you've taken delivery and the dealer is no longer responsible for missing accessories.
- [ ] Wait for the dealer to do a thorough dealer preparation.
- [ ] Inspect your car both inside and out.
- [ ] Take a second test drive.
- [ ] When buying a used car, *do not* be in a hurry!
- [ ] Test drive a used car to determine whether it is safe.
- [ ] Ask why the former owner is selling it.
- [ ] Call the previous owner to verify mileage and condition.
- [ ] Sit in all seats to evaluate leg and head room.
- [ ] Examine outside of the car for rust, dents, and evidence of damage and repair.
- [ ] Make sure all promises are in writing.
- [ ] Check details of warranty.
- [ ] Find out if parts and service are readily available.
- [ ] Find out who will do the service. An authorized dealer?
- [ ] Have your own mechanic check the car at his place of business, or have it checked at a diagnostic center. Inspect:
  - Brakes
  - Carpeting
  - Safety belts
  - Upholstery
  - Oil dipstick for dirty oil
  - Battery
  - Belts and hoses
  - Leaking fluid
  - Windows
  - Test all lights
  - Suspension
  - Steering
  - Running gear
  - Cooling system
  - Transmission
  - Body
  - Frame
  - Tires—including the spare
  - Is it level? (shocks)

CAR CARE

- [ ] Inflate tires to recommended pressure; but do not overinflate.
- [ ] Keep and use tire guarantees.
- [ ] Keep tires balanced and aligned.
- [ ] Buy tires in pairs or fours so that they wear evenly.
- [ ] Consider radial tires for improved gas mileage.
- [ ] A good quality retread tire is frequently a better buy than a cheap, second- or third-line new tire. But don't buy used tires or regrooves.
- [ ] Have brakes adjusted to be sure they grip and release properly.
- [ ] To protect your car while it's parked, set brakes, turn wheels toward curb, and lock all doors.
- [ ] Shop for car insurance, comparing coverage for your individual needs.
- [ ] Clean off the top of the battery and check connections every six months.
- [ ] Buy a lifetime battery only if you plan to keep the car more than five years.
- [ ] Use the gasoline octane and oil grade recommended for your car.

- ☐ Take the used oil to your service station for recycling.
- ☐ Buy oil by the case when on sale.
- ☐ To get true oil reading, check oil at home in the garage or on a level place when the engine is cold.
- ☐ Good preventive maintenance pays off in less corrective maintenance.
- ☐ Have your car tuned regularly—every 5,000 miles.
- ☐ Check spark plugs every 10,000 miles.
- ☐ Cleaning points or replacing them when required saves gas and oil.
- ☐ Keep the engine filters clean.
- ☐ Wash and wax your car yourself—frequent washing and waxing helps prevent rust.
- ☐ Keep mileage records for the following: medical care, business or charitable driving, car damage or loss, interest on car payments.

INSURANCE

- ☐ Pay insurance premiums annually for lowest cost.
- ☐ Accept policies with higher deductibles for lower premiums.
- ☐ Update your insurance regularly.
- ☐ Install and maintain at least one smoke detector in your home.
- ☐ Take time to make a complete household inventory.
- ☐ Repair loose handrails and carpets to avoid accidents.
- ☐ Keep fire extinguisher in kitchen.
- ☐ Teach children about proper use of matches, lighters, and flammable liquids.
- ☐ Keep trash, paper, and rag accumulation to a minimum.
- ☐ Store flammable paints and fuels away from pilot lights and out from under stairways.
- ☐ Keep area around furnace and hot water heater clear for air circulation.
- ☐ If you have children, keep medicine, poison, and matches locked out of children's reach.
- ☐ Keep emergency phone numbers posted by the telephone.

HEALTH

- ☐ Eat well—less meat, oil, and sugar; more grains, fruits, and vegetables.
- ☐ Get the right amount of sleep.
- ☐ Exercise every day.
- ☐ Drink lots of water.
- ☐ Maintain proper body weight.
- ☐ Make sure immunizations are up to date.
- ☐ Cut down or eliminate tobacco and alcohol.
- ☐ Have regular dental and medical checkups.
- ☐ Brush and floss teeth twice daily—as though you were on your way to see your dentist.
- ☐ Buy health supplies and toiletries at discount stores rather than drugstores.
- ☐ Ask your doctor about generic drugs.
- ☐ Compare prescription prices at various drug stores.
- ☐ Make your own first-aid kit instead of buying a ready-made kit.
- ☐ Keep on hand simple remedies and antibiotic creams.
- ☐ Have some form of health insurance, through group plan if possible.
- ☐ Keep paramedic and fire department phone numbers in plain sight.
- ☐ Donate blood for someone else and get future credit for yourself and family.
- ☐ Visit doctors at office rather than having them come to your home.
- ☐ Call doctor before making an appointment to see if a visit is necessary.

- ☐ Have medical and dental X rays transferred when moving or changing doctors.
- ☐ Watch for community health services and screening programs.
- ☐ Keep *accurate* records of the following for future use:
  - Illnesses
  - Immunization
  - X rays
  - Accidents
  - Hospitalization
  - Diagnostic tests
  - Treatment
  - Physical therapy
  - Include name of doctor, date and place of treatment

TRAVEL

- ☐ Work through a good travel agent, as he has price comparisons readily available.
- ☐ Midweek rates are often less than weekend rates.
- ☐ Round-trip tickets are sometimes less than two one-way fares.
- ☐ Vacation when others don't—off season, just before, or just after crowds.
- ☐ Go with a group.
- ☐ Consider a pre-package vacation plan.
- ☐ Contact the chamber of commerce of destination and intermittent stops for free vacation information.
- ☐ Join a travel club.
- ☐ Look into tour or travel passes—bus, train, plane.
- ☐ Investigate swapping houses with someone in the area you want to visit.
- ☐ Camp out in a tent or trailer. Compare costs for rental and buying.
- ☐ Some national parks have rustic cabins available for minimal cost.
- ☐ Advance reservations often cost less than on-arrival reservations.
- ☐ Take your bicycle along—it can be shipped on an airplane, bus, or train.
- ☐ It pays to compare motel costs. There are some budget motels with no frills.
- ☐ Tourist homes offering bed and breakfast are available in some areas.
- ☐ Watch for coupons in travel guides, magazines, and books.

RESIDENTIAL ENERGY

Heating and cooling	70%
Water heating	20%
Lighting, cooking, running small appliances	10%

- ☐ Heating and cooling offer your best opportunities to save energy money. All utility companies now offer a low-cost audit service to evaluate home energy and to make suggestions.
- ☐ Consider insulating exterior walls. Warning—this can be costly.
- ☐ Insulate floors over unheated spaces such as crawl spaces, porches, and garages.
- ☐ Test your windows and doors for airtightness. Caulk and weatherstrip doors and windows. It is easy to do yourself!
- ☐ Install storm windows and doors. (Less expensive alternatives range from heavy-duty, clear plastic sheets on a frame, to clear plastic film which can be taped lightly to the inside of the window frames.)
- ☐ Close off closets and unoccupied rooms and shut their vents.
- ☐ Use kitchen, bath, and other ventilating fans sparingly.
- ☐ Keep your fireplace damper closed unless you have a fire going. Glass fireplace screens also help.

- [ ] Lower the thermostat at night or consider the advantages of a clock thermostat.
- [ ] Do not block air or heat ducts with furniture or drapes.
- [ ] Insulate ducts.
- [ ] Turn down thermostat while away from home all day or on vacation.
- [ ] Plant deciduous trees on south and west sides of the home to provide shade in the summer and sunshine in the winter.
- [ ] Turn the furnace down to 55° when burning a fire in the fireplace unless the fireplace is vented from the outside.
- [ ] Lower your thermostat to 65° during the day and 55° at night.
- [ ] Using an electric blanket at night on a medium setting costs 4¢ a night.
- [ ] Have your oil furnace serviced at least once a year, preferably each summer to take advantage of off-season rates.
- [ ] Clean or replace the filter in your forced-air heating system each month.
- [ ] Check the ductwork for air leaks about once a year if you have a forced-air heating system. When the fan is running, feel around the duct joints for escaping air.
- [ ] If you have oil heat, have your serviceman check to see if the firing rate is correct. A recent survey found that 97% of the furnaces checked were over-fired.
- [ ] Don't let cold air seep into your home through the attic access door. Be sure it is well insulated and weather-stripped.
- [ ] Dust or vacuum radiator surfaces frequently.
- [ ] Keep draperies and shades open in sunny windows; close them at night.
- [ ] For comfort in cooler indoor temperatures, wear warm clothing.
- [ ] If you need central air conditioning, select a unit with the lowest suitable capacity and highest efficiency.
- [ ] Make sure the ducts in your air conditioning system are properly insulated, especially those that pass through the attic or other uncooled spaces.
- [ ] If you don't need central air conditioning, consider using individual window or through-the-wall units. As a rule, these cost less to buy and operate.
- [ ] Install a whole-house ventilating fan in your attic or in an upstairs window to cool the house when it's cool outside.
- [ ] Set your thermostat at no less than 78° F in the summer.
- [ ] Clean or replace air conditioning filters at least once a month. When the filter is dirty, the fan has to run longer to move the same amount of air.
- [ ] Turn off your window air conditioners when you leave a room for several hours.
- [ ] If your air conditioner is strong enough to cool additional space, consider using a fan with your window air conditioner to spread the cooled air farther.
- [ ] Do not place lamps or TV sets near your air conditioning thermostat.
- [ ] If you live in a warm climate, remember that light-colored roofing can help keep the house cooler.
- [ ] Keep out daytime sun with vertical louvers or awnings on the outside of your windows, or draw draperies, blinds, and shades indoors.
- [ ] Keep lights low or off during the summer. Electric lights generate heat.
- [ ] Do your cooking and use other heat-generating appliances in the early morning and late evening hours whenever possible.
- [ ] Open the windows instead of using your air conditioner or electric fan on cooler days and during cooler hours.
- [ ] Consider turning off the furnace pilot light in summer, but don't forget to relight it when cold weather arrives.
- [ ] Dress for warmer indoor temperatures by wearing lightweight, open-weave fabrics.
- [ ] Be sure to keep windows, drapes, and outside doors closed during the hottest hours of the day.
- [ ] Use window or whole-house ventilating fans to cool the house when it's cool outside.
- [ ] Use vents and exhaust fans to pull heat and moisture from the attic, kitchen, and laundry directly to the outside.
- [ ] Turn off lights in any room not being used.
- [ ] Reduce overall lighting in non-working spaces by removing one bulb out of three in multiple light fixtures and replacing it with a burned-out bulb for safety.
- [ ] Replace other bulbs throughout the house with bulbs of the next lower wattage.
- [ ] Install solid state dimmers or hi-low switches.
- [ ] Use one large bulb instead of several small ones in areas where bright light is needed.
- [ ] Use low-wattage night-light bulbs.
- [ ] Use fluorescent lights whenever you can.
- [ ] Keep all lamps and lighting fixtures clean. Dirt absorbs light.
- [ ] Save on lighting energy by using light colors, especially on the ceiling, because they reflect the light and reduce the amount of artificial light required.
- [ ] Have decorative outdoor gas lamps turned off unless they are essential for safety, or convert them to electricity.
- [ ] Use outdoor lights only when they are needed.
- [ ] As an activity to show family members how much electricity even one light uses, have family members watch electricity meter while one person turns on and later off a bedroom light or the bathroom fan. Then explain how each unit is measured and the monetary charge for it.

More
Help

He that buys what he does not want,
will soon want what he cannot buy.

Our federal government offers a wide array of free and inexpensive pamphlets. The printing office puts out a new catalogue every three months describing pertinent material. Various other agencies, such as the Internal Revenue Service, put out additional specific details from their jurisdictions. Following is a sample list of topics. Send for the free catalogue, and watch for new information. When the materials are free, a post card is enough for your request. Remember to ALWAYS include your ZIP code with the return address.

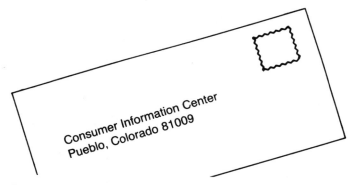

Consumer Information Center
Pueblo, Colorado 81009

Examples of free pamphlets:
Consumer Information Catalog
   (Free catalog printed every three or four months listing current pamphlets from various agencies.)
Consumer Resource Handbook
   (Can help you locate the best sources of information and help offered by businesses, industry groups, volunteer organizations, government, labor organizations, and the media.)
A New Car Buying Guide
Buying a Used Car
Keeping Records—What to Discard

Self-Evaluation

While some people are waiting for their ship to come in, others build one.

Rate yourself from 1 to 10 points on each question, with 10 being the highest possible score, to pinpoint successes and weaknesses to be worked on.

____ Members of my household are satisfied with our present standard of living.
____ Installment payments are not more than 20% of income.
____ Everyone has some say about goals.
____ Everyone is helping and cooperating in ways to reach goals, such as turning off lights and cutting gasoline consumption.
____ I am making some progress toward long-term goals.
____ I have at least one month's salary in emergency savings.
____ Expenses are less than income.
____ I buy according to plan rather than on impulse.
____ I pay my debts when due.
____ I have good feelings of being in control of finances.
____ I know exactly where the money is going.
____ Arguments over money are at a minimum.
____ The checking account is balanced every month.
____ I balance the monthly expense charts in this book every month.
____ Expenses are estimated quite accurately.
____ Checks are written only when money is in the account to cover them.
____ I save something regularly.
____ I can afford what I want or my wants are within my means.
____ I seldom regret what I buy.
____ I have an up-to-date will.
____ I have an accurate home inventory.
____ A place has been set up to file bills, receipts, and other financial papers.
____ I maintain a safe-deposit box.
____ I keep accurate records during the year for income taxes.
____ My health, life, car, and property insurance are adequate.
____ I have recorded names, numbers, and addresses of all credit cards.
____ I seldom have to pay service charges for credit card accounts.
____ I have a good credit rating.
____ I have developed a budget I feel comfortable with.
____ I seem to have more money left over to buy the things I want.

200–250: You're doing great! Keep up the good work.
150–200: You have a good start, but keep trying harder.
Under 150: Reread this book!